Get Your Tax Back!

First published in 2011 by
Liberties Press
Guinness Enterprise Centre | Taylor's Lane | Dublin 8
Tel: +353 (1) 415 1224
www.LibertiesPress.com | info@libertiespress.com

Distributed in the United States by
Dufour Editions | PO Box 7 | Chester Springs | Pennsylvania | 19425

and in Australia by
James Bennett Pty Limited | InBooks | 3 Narabang Way
Belrose NSW 2085

Trade enquiries to Gill & Macmillan Distribution
Hume Avenue | Park West | Dublin 12
Tel: +353 (1) 500 9534 | Fax: +353 (1) 500 9595
sales@gillmacmillan.ie

ISBN: 978–1–907593–09–3
2 4 6 8 10 9 7 5 3 1

A CIP record for this title is available from the British Library.

Cover design by Ros Murphy
Internal design by Liberties Press
Printed in Ireland by Colour Books

Author royalties from sales of this book will be donated to

THE CHILDREN'S MEDICAL & RESEARCH FOUNDATION
OUR LADY'S CHILDREN'S HOSPITAL, CRUMLIN

Get Your Tax Back!

The Irish Guide to Unlocking Your Allowances

Aidan Kelly

with additional material by Orla Riddell

LIB
ERT
IES

Contents

‘A book . . . is a living and breathing document that grows richer with each new reading.’

MALCOLM GLADWELL

Acknowledgements

To Luke, Danny and Jess. Thanks for making sure I start each day with a smile on my face.

To my great parents Pat and Gerry, for all their love, help and friendship over the years.

To my family, especially my brother Gerard, for your help and inspiration, and my friends, in particular Jarlath.

To Sue my wife for all your love, support and belief. You truly are the most special person.

Note on Tax Efficient Giving

Anyone making a donation to the Children's Medical & Research Foundation, Our Lady's Hospital for Sick Children, Crumlin, who is a taxpayer and who donated €250 or more in a year will be able to either allow the charity to reclaim that tax or, if you are self-employed or a corporate donor, you will be able to claim back the tax yourself.

From 6 April 2001, tax relief was made available on donations of €250 or more in any one tax year to eligible charities from both individual and corporate donors. Tax relief is applied to these donations at the donor's marginal rate of tax.

In the case of PAYE taxpayers, the tax relief is applied at the marginal rate and is paid directly by the Revenue Commissioners to the eligible charity or approved body on receipt of the relevant 'appropriate certificate' (an official form that is supplied by the charity, completed by the donor and returned to the charity receiving the donation).

EXAMPLE

PAYE DONOR (HIGHER RATE)

Joe is a PAYE taxpayer who donated €254 to the Children's Medical & Research Foundation. His marginal rate of tax is 41 percent. As Joe has already paid tax, his donation is made from his net income. Joe completes the 'appropriate certificate' supplied to him by the Children's Medical & Research Foundation, giving details of his donation and PPS number, and returns it to the foundation. The foundation then uses the form to claim back from the Revenue the tax which Joe has already paid on the €254.

€254 is 58 percent of what Joe earned.
€254 x 100/58 = €437 (Gross earnings)
€437 - €254 = €183 (already paid in tax to the revenue)

€183 is what the Children's Medical & Research Foundation can reclaim back from the revenue. The value of Joe's donation then increases to €437 (€254 + €183).

SELF-EMPLOYED
Individual taxpayers on self-assessment benefit directly from relief at the marginal rate by claiming the donation as a tax-deductible expense.

EXAMPLE
Anne is self-employed and makes her returns on a self-assessment basis. Her marginal rate of tax is 42 percent. Anne donates €254 to the Children's Medical & Research Foundation. Anne receives a receipt from the charity and, when she completes her tax return, she deducts the donation of €254 from her taxable income, thus reducing her tax bill by €106.

CORPORATE DONORS
Corporate donors can simply claim a deduction for the donation as if it were a trading expense.

Points to note:
To qualify for the tax relief, a donation must satisfy a number of conditions:

- It must be in the form of money
- It must not be repayable

- It must not confer any benefit on the donor or any person connected with the donor
- It must not be conditional on, or associated with, any arrangement involving the acquisition of property by the charity or approved body.

An eligible charity is defined by the legislation as any charity within the State which is authorised in writing by the Revenue Commissioners for the purpose of this scheme. In order to qualify for eligible charity state, the charitable organisation must:

- have a charitable tax exemption number or CHY number
- be in operation for at least three years since being granted the CHY number
- make a formal application to the Revenue on the form of 'application to Revenue for Authorisation as an Eligible Charity for the purposes of Section 45, Finance Act, 2001 (donations to eligible charities)'

Introduction

Welcome to *Get Your Tax Back!*, the book that will give you all the information you need to claim all the tax reliefs that are due to you and do your own yearly personal tax assessment.

The idea for this book came to me about a year ago. In a previous job, I worked in an office and one of my jobs there was organising the payroll and wages. It was through this experience that I learned how to calculate how much tax a person should be paying and also what were the various ways of paying less tax. Every year, when the employees received their P60, there was a discrepancy between the tax they had paid and the tax that they should have paid. I found this true for myself also and started checking the P60 of all the employees every year and helping them get their tax back. In most cases the amount repaid was about €100 but, as the taxation system is not an exact science, every person was entitled to some repayment, no matter how small! Over the years I have always checked my own P60 along with that of family, friends and work colleagues. On some occasions there were large amounts of money repaid, for which I was promised drinks and dinner for my help. Some have lived up to their promises – those of you who didn't, you know who you are.

Taxation and dealing with the Revenue office can sometimes be quite daunting for people. I am not an accountant and neither do you need to be to understand this book.

Yes, there are parts which require some calculations, but the main aim of the book is to give you the all the information available so that you can claim all that you are entitled to.

In December, we were presented with what many commentators called the toughest budget in recent memory. Since the onset of the recession, people have become more concerned about the money they spend and the ways in which they can save money. The majority of people in this country pay their tax through the Pay As You Earn system (PAYE).This book is aimed mainly at them. Their employer calculates their wages and deducts the tax and PRSI based on figures which are supplied to them by the employee or the tax office. But what if this information is wrong? What if the tax office is not aware that you recently got married, are a member of a trade union or are paying medical insurance? There are many different ways that a person can qualify for tax relief. The onus is on each individual to make sure that they claim all the reliefs that they are entitled to.

At present, there are companies which will take your details and process your claim for you – at a cost! Alternatively, there is the free service offered by the Revenue Commissioners, again where you supply the information. But what if you are not aware of what you might be entitled to? The main reason for writing this book is that, through my research into both services, I noticed major flaws. A person may make a claim for the current year and also, retrospectively, for the previous four years. So in total, you can claim for five years. During this period of time, many people's circumstances change from year to year. Also, if you are not fully aware of the reliefs which are available to you, how can you make a proper claim? The main aim of the book is to show you exactly what tax you should be paying and, more importantly, what reliefs are available.

During the course of the book, I will show you who qualifies for each relief and how to claim them. I plan to explain each section to you and then give the formula you can use to calculate what reliefs are due to you. All information here has been sourced through the Revenue Commissioners and is presented to you in a user-friendly way. All rates specified in the book were the current rates at time of publication.

The book is organised into two parts. The first part deals with the rules of taxation and the various ways in which they apply to each person's circumstances. It also outlines what tax a person is liable for and the rates and formulae which can be used to calculate their tax liability. I explain the many terms which are used and show you the various ways in which a person may reduce their tax liability. I have also included information about the recent income levy tax and how people who have been made redundant or subject to emergency tax can claim any overpaid tax which may be due to them. We also examine the most commonly used forms, such as your tax credits certificate, P45 and P60 forms and look at how we can use each to make sure that we are claiming and paying the correct amount of tax.

The second part of the book sets out all the reliefs that are available to people – reliefs that will add to their personal tax credits and further reduce their tax liability. These have been categorised as other personal reliefs and include: widowed person's relief; home carer's relief; age tax credit; income tax exemption; marginal relief; relief for tuition fees; blind person's relief; incapacitated child relief and dependent relative credit. I also examine work-related reliefs, such as reliefs for trade union subscriptions, childcare service providers and those who receive Revenue Job Assist.

In the chapter on housing-related reliefs, I look at ways of claiming relief for service charges, such as domestic bin charges and water rates, and reliefs available for both people who rent accommodation and landlords. For home-owners, I look at mortgage interest relief and interest relief on loans for house improvements.

Finally, I examine the reliefs available for medical expenses and dental expenses, for medical insurance premiums, and for approved permanent health benefit schemes. Each section will be explained fully, and the amount of relief available and how each relief can be claimed will be presented in a step-by-step, easy-to-understand way. I will also give you contact details for each local Revenue office, where you can send your claims, along with details of the application form relevant to each claim.

This book is guaranteed to save you money, can be used over and over again, and is suitable for everyone - taxi drivers, doctors, gardaí, nurses, IT workers, and anyone who wants to save money. Also, people who have been subject to Emergency Tax, who have been made redundant or who previously may not have worked for some part of a year can calculate their tax liability and check for any refunds which may be due to them. There are also a number of reliefs that may be claimed retrospectively which you may not qualify for now but were entitled to claim for previously. Also, if you have made a claim in the last few years and were unaware of some of the reliefs that you were entitled to, you may still be able to claim these.

On 6 April 2001, tax credits replaced the old system of tax-free allowances. The annual tax year now runs from 1 January to 31 December. This is the system that is used to calculate the amount of tax paid each week. The starting point for all workers is their personal tax credits for the year. This is based on personal circumstances and gross income. There are two tax bands - the lower of the two, commonly referred to as the standard rate, and the upper limit, commonly referred to as the higher rate. Tax bands relating to an individual's personal circumstances give the cut-off point to which a person pays the standard rate. After this point, the higher rate of tax applies. Once you have established your gross pay less any deductions for pension contributories, you can then calculate what tax, minus your tax credit, should be paid.

There is no need to worry about the intricacies of this, as all will be explained and shown in step-by-step, practical terms during the course of this book. More than 60 percent of people do not claim their full entitlement in respect of reliefs due to them. Now is the time to learn exactly what you are entitled to, and to claim back the money that is rightly yours. Once you do this once, you will have the knowledge and ability to do it year after year. It's your money – get your tax back!

Regards, and many thanks,

Aidan Kelly

1

Personal Tax Credits

At the start of every year, the Revenue office will issue each person with a tax credit certificate. The information contained on this certificate is based on the personal information which is on file at the Revenue offices. This information would normally consist of the following personal details of a person: name, address, age, marital status, and current employer. If you have not received a certificate of tax credits, you must complete and forward form 12A to your local tax office. *Likewise if these circumstances on your tax credits certificate are not correct, it is important that you inform the Revenue office as soon as possible so that you get your full tax relief.* This can be done by contacting your local Revenue office in person or by phone or post. Similarly, if your circumstances change during the year, you should inform your local Revenue office as soon as possible. Below is the information needed to make sure that the figure on the tax relief certificate you receive matches what you are entitled to. In all dealings with the Revenue office, you will need to quote your PPS number.

PPS Number

A Personal Public Service number (PPS number) is an individual's unique identification number for all dealings with the public service, including Social Welfare, tax, education and health services. Most Irish nationals born in Ireland after 1971 and registered for tax since 1979 have been issued with a PPS number. Likewise, those who have claimed social welfare or been issued with a Social Services card would probably have a PPS number.

If you do not hold a PPS number, you must first register with the Department of Social and Family Affairs by:

- calling in person to a Department of Social and Family Affairs Local Office
- completing a PPS number application, Form REG 1
- presenting documentary evidence as requested in the application form to verify your identity (long version of birth certificate, passport or driving licence). Non-Irish nationals will be required to provide their 'green card'.

You will be notified of your PPS number when a Social Services card is issued to you. Your PPS number is very important and you should keep a permanent record of it. Always quote the number when writing or calling to your Revenue office, or to the Department of Social and Family Affairs. This will avoid unnecessary delays.

Personal tax credits are the credits that each person is entitled to at the beginning of every tax year: 1 January. Each person qualifies for a personal tax credit, the amount of which depends on whether a person is married or single. However, if you are married, there are different ways of allocating the relief, as you will see. The current rates are as follows:

Single Person's Tax Credit:	€1,650
Married Person's Tax Credit:	€3,300

The figure above for the married person's tax credit applies where a married couple are assessed jointly and one of the couple, usually the higher earner, takes the tax credit for both persons.

Single person's tax credit

As the name suggests, this is the figure that each single person, not married or separated, qualifies for and is the figure which should appear on their certificate of tax credits. In the case of the single person's tax credit, if you get married, both you and your spouse continue to be treated as single people for tax purposes in that year. *If, however, the tax you pay as two single people is greater than that which would be payable if you were taxed as a married couple, you can claim any refund you may be entitled to.*

If you are recently married, refunds are only due from the date of marriage and will be calculated after the following 31 December. So, for example, if you were married in 2009, any tax refund due to you will be calculated after 31 December 2009. If you got married in 2010, any tax refund due to you will be calculated after 31 December 2010. Refunds are normally only due where a couple are taxed at different rates and one spouse could benefit from the unused standard rate cut-off point, or for some of the unused tax credits of the other spouse. So if you get married, it is important to advise the tax office of the date of your marriage. You will also need to quote your own and your spouse's PPS numbers.

The single person's tax credit is currently €1,650 and, as we will soon see, this added to a person's PAYE credit, also €1,650, will be the basis of his/her tax relief credits.

Married person's tax credit

For the years which follow your marriage, there are three options available for the taxation of married people. All of the options, and the benefits of choosing each one, are outlined and explained below. The three options available to married persons are as follows:

- assessment as a single person (i.e. you are both still taxed as single people)

- separate assessment
- joint assessment/aggregation

Rules and Different Types of Assessment

Assessment as a single person

If you are married, you can continue to be assessed as a single person. This will apply to both you and your spouse. Your tax affairs are completely separate and you will each receive the single person's tax credit. Any unused tax credits may not be transferred, nor can tax credits which may ordinarily have been divided between spouses. Your relief will be based on the current single person's allowance, and this is the figure that will appear on your tax credits certificate.

Separate assessment

Under the separate assessment option, the tax affairs of spouses are independent of each other. However, the difference between separate assessment and the previous option (assessment as a single person) is that under this option, some tax credits are divided equally between you. These tax credits are:

- married tax credit
- age tax credit
- blind person's tax credit
- incapacitated child tax credit

The balance of the tax credits is given to each of you in proportion to the cost borne by each. The PAYE tax credit and expenses (if any) are allocated to the appropriate spouse. Any tax credits other than the PAYE tax credit and employment expenses that are unused by one partner can be claimed by the other spouse. The tax credits are not usually adjusted until after the end of the tax year. Any credits that are unused (other than the PAYE tax credit and employment expenses) and the standard rate cut-off point, up to €41,800 in 2011, and €45,400 in 2010 and 2009, can be transferred to the other spouse, but only at the end of the tax year. The increase in the standard rate tax band of up to €23,800 in 2011 and €27,400 in 2010 and 2009 is not transferrable between partners. If you think you have unused tax credits or have not reached the standard rate cut-off point, contact your tax office for a review after the end of the tax year. Overall, the amount of the tax that is payable under this option (separate assessment) is the same as that payable under the joint assessment option discussed below.

To claim the separate assessment option, you must do so in writing. The claim must be made in the period between 1 October and 31 March and cannot be backdated. This option remains until either one of you contacts your local tax office and informs them that you want to change your circumstances. Either spouse can make an application for this form of assessment. To withdraw the option, you must contact your tax office in writing. Each spouse can complete a separate return of his or her own income. Your tax office will, however, accept a joint return (which either of you can make) if the joint return includes the income of both spouses.

Joint assessment

The joint assessment (or 'aggregation') option is usually the most common and certainly the most favourable basis of assessment for a married couple. *This assessment is automatically given by the tax office when you advise them of your marriage, but this does not prevent you from choosing either of the options that we have examined earlier.*

Under this option, the tax credits and standard rate cut-off point can be allocated between spouses to suit their circumstances. If only one spouse has taxable income, all tax credits and the standard rate cut-off point will be given to the spouse with the income. If both of you have taxable income, you can decide which of you is to be the assessable spouse. You then ask the tax office to allocate the tax credits and standard rate cut-off point between the two of you in whatever way you wish. Note: The PAYE tax credit, employment expenses, and the increase in the standard rate cut-off point of €23,800 in 2011 and €27,400 in 2010 and 2009 are not transferrable.

It is important to note that if your tax office does not get a request from you to allocate your tax credits in any particular way, the tax office will normally give all the tax credits (apart from the other partner's PAYE and expense tax credits) to the spouse being assessed. The spouse who is not being assessed still qualifies for their PAYE tax credit and also any other reliefs to which they may be entitled. The spouse being assessed must complete the return of income for the couple and is charged tax on the joint income of the couple.

Can joint assessment apply where one of the spouses is self employed?

Yes. If one spouse is self-employed, joint assessment can still apply but not if both are self-employed. The flexibility this option brings can be very convenient - especially if one of you pays tax under the PAYE system and the other pays tax under the self-assessment system. Under joint assessment, you let your circumstances determine whether most of the tax should be paid under PAYE or in a lump sum on assessment. This is determined by the way in which the tax credits are allocated. If you choose to pay most of your tax under PAYE, the tax credits (apart from the PAYE tax credit and employment expenses) should be offset against the self-assessment income.

The choice about who becomes the assessable spouse is made by both of you. All you need to do is to inform Revenue which of you is to be the assessable spouse. You should make your nomination before the end of the tax year (31 December) to ensure that the correct tax credits and standard rate cut-off point are allocated to each spouse from the start of the tax year. If you have not made your nomination, the spouse with the higher income in the latest year for which details of both spouses' incomes are known becomes the assessable spouse. This person continues to be so until both of you jointly elect that the other spouse is to be the assessable spouse or until either of you opts for either separate assessment or assessment as a single person.

Repayments of Tax

Repayments that arise from an end-of-year review will in general be apportioned on the basis of the tax paid by each spouse. If both of you are in employment, then, as we have seen, a Certificate of Tax Credits is issued to each of you. All of the tax credits and reliefs due to a married couple where joint assessment applies are shown on the assessable spouse's notice: the amount 'allocated to other employments' is also shown. This amount represents the tax credits that are allocated to the other spouse and may also include tax credits from a subsidiary employment or pension of either spouse.

Married Tax Rates

The standard rate cut-off point for married couples is €41,800 in 2011 and €45,400 in 2010 and 2009. This amount is taxed at 20 percent, and the balance is taxed at 41 percent. Where both spouses have income, this standard rate cut-off point can be increased by the *lower* of the following:

- €23,800 in 2011 or
- the amount of the income of the spouse with the smaller income.

The increase in the standard rate cut-off point interacts with the Home Carer's Tax Credit. If the increased standard rate cut-off point is more beneficial than the Home Carer's Tax Credit, you can claim the increase instead. As a matter of course, the tax office will grant you whichever is more beneficial to you. The rules governing the calculation of relief for Home Carer's Tax Credit will be explained in full later in the book: see the section on the Home Carer's Tax Credit.

PAYE Tax Credit

As we saw earlier, each person receives a tax credit relating to whether they are married or single (or married and assessed as a single person). Also, each person, whether married or single, will also receive a PAYE tax credit unless they are self-employed. This credit is not transferrable and only applies where a person is in employment and paying income tax.

The current PAYE tax relief rate is €1,650. If we now add the earlier figure for our personal tax credit and our PAYE tax credit, this is the starting figure for our personal tax credits, before we add any reliefs which we may qualify for. See below:

Personal tax credit in step 1 + PAYE relief = personal tax relief credits

EXAMPLE 1
€1,650 + €1,650 = €3,300: single person's starting point for relief or married person assessed separately or as a single person.

EXAMPLE 2
€3,300 + €1,650 = €4,950: married person's starting point for relief in cases where they are assessed jointly. (*This rate*

is given to one spouse - usually the higher earner of the two. The other spouse will still qualify for their PAYE allowance of €1,650.)

2

Tax Rates and Tax Bands

In this section, we will look at the existing tax rates and bands which relate to both married and single persons. I will also explain some of the terms used and how the tax rates and bands are applied, and will give you the formula necessary for calculating your tax liability. We will also look at how investing in a pension or AVC (Additional Voluntary Contribution) can actually reduce the amount of tax you are liable to pay. Tax rates and tax bands give us the formula and criteria to calculate the amount of tax to be paid on a person's gross pay before we apply tax relief. Tax rates are the rates payable on a person's gross pay. They are divided into two sections, commonly referred to as the Standard Rate and Higher Rate.

Standard Rate

The standard rate of tax is the lower of the two tax rates. It is the rate that you pay tax at up to the limit that is set for that year (2011 figures put the standard rate of tax at 20 percent).

Higher Rate

The higher rate of tax is the rate of tax you pay once your income has exceeded or is likely to exceed the standard rate. The higher rate, as the name suggests, is the rate which begins where the standard rate stops. (2011 figures put the higher rate of tax at 41 percent)

Cut-off Points

Cut-off points are the points at which the different tax rates (standard and higher) apply. The standard rate of tax applies to all earnings up to the cut-off point; above this point, the higher rate of tax applies. The cut-off point will probably change from year to year, and from budget to budget, so make sure you have the figure you require for the relevant period.

Gross Pay/Net Pay

Gross pay is the figure for a person's salary before any deductions are made. It can also apply to the figure that remains after pension contributions, which are allowable for income tax, are deducted.

Net pay is the figure which remains after all tax and deductions have been made. This is also referred to as your take-home pay.

Tax Bands

As you will see below, the tax bands are divided into four categories. Two relate to a single person and two relate to a married person.

Single/widowed without dependent children
2011 figure: €32,800 @ 20 percent, balance @ 41 percent

This band relates to a single or widowed person without any dependent children. The band allows a single person (at current rates - check figures for the period you require) to earn up to €32,800 and pay tax on this income at 20 percent (the standard rate). Above this limit of €32,800, a person will pay tax at 41 percent (the higher rate).

Single/widowed qualifying for One-Parent Tax Credit
2011 figure: €36,800 @ 20 percent, balance @ 41 percent

This band relates to a single or widowed person who qualifies for one parent tax credit (explained on page 69). This band allows a single person (at current rates - check figures for the period you require) to earn up to €36,800 and pay tax on this income at 20 percent (the standard rate). Above this limit of €36,800, a person will pay tax at 41 percent (the higher rate).

Married couple – one spouse with income
2011 figure - €41,800 @ 20 percent, balance @ 41 percent

This band relates to a couple where only one of the spouses has an income. This band allows the assessable spouse (at current rates - check figures for the period you require) to earn up to €41,800 and pay tax on this income at 20 percent (the standard rate). Above this limit of €41,800, a person will pay tax at 41 percent (the higher rate).

Married couple – both spouses with income
2011 figure - €41,800 @ 20 percent (with a maximum increase of €23,800 - see below), balance @ 41 percent

This band relates to a married couple where both spouses are working. The band allows the assessable spouse (at current rates - check figures for the period you require) to earn up to €41,800 and pay tax on this income at 20 percent (the standard rate). It also allows the assessable spouse to earn up to another €23,800, which is payable at the standard rate of tax. Therefore, the assessable spouse in cases where both spouses are working and paying tax can earn up to €65,600, paying tax at the standard rate, before the higher rate applies. It is important to note that if this limit is not reached, the allowance cannot be transferred and used by the non-assessable spouse.

How to Calculate Your Tax Liability

When calculating your tax liability, the figures may change through the years, and over the various budgets, but the formula is always the same. Just take whichever band, described above, applies to you and insert the cut-off point. Calculate the rate of tax due up to the cut-off point by taking the standard rate as a percentage of the cut-off point. You must use the higher rate to calculate the tax due on any income above the cut-off point.

The formulae

To calculate the rate percentage, convert the tax rate to a decimal number, eg:

100 percent = 1
20 percent (standard rate) = 0.2
41 percent (higher rate) = 0.41

If your income *does not exceed* the cut-off point which relates to you, calculate the current standard rate percentage of your income.

Salary x Standard Rate percentage = Tax liability

From the figure of tax liability, subtract your Personal Tax Credit and PAYE credit to give the amount of tax that is payable.

Tax liability - (Personal Tax Credit + PAYE Credit) = Tax payable

If your income *exceeds* the cut-off point, it is necessary to complete three calculations to calculate your tax liability.

The first is to assess tax liability at the standard rate. To do this, subtract the relevant cut-off point from your salary and multiply the remainder by the standard percentage rate of tax. The second calculation is to assess the tax liability at the higher rate above the cut-off point. Similarly, with the balance of salary above the cut-off point, multiply it by the current higher percentage rate of tax. Thirdly, add the results from each calculation to give the figure for tax liability. The following formula should be applied:

(Cut–off point x Standard rate percentage) + (Salary - Cut–off point x Higher rate percentage) = Tax liability

From the figure of tax liability, subtract your Personal Tax Credit and PAYE credit to give the tax that is payable.

Tax liability - Personal Tax Credit and PAYE credit = Tax payable

Select the band which relates to you and input your figures to get your tax liability. Remember: the formula is always the same - the only figures that change are the following:

- Figure for your earnings
- Figure for cut-off point
- Tax rates for standard and higher rates
- Figure for personal tax relief as per your circumstances

As we will see, it is also possible to reduce the amount of salary which is liable to tax, at either the standard or higher rate, by deducting pension contributions from the salary.

Below are some practical examples of how the formulae are applied. In each case we can calculate the tax liability. However it is important to note that this is the figure *before* any reliefs or pension contributions are applied. Do not worry about this too much at this point; everything will be explained as we go along.

EXAMPLE 1

The yearly salary of Gerry, a single man, is €32,500. Multiply Gerry's salary by the standard rate only, as Gerry does not exceed the band for the standard rate. This will give us his tax liability for the year.

32,500 x 0.20 = 6,500

The figure of €6,500 is Gerry's tax liability for the year before tax reliefs are applied. This figure of €6,500 is got by multiplying €32,500 (Gerry's salary) by 20 percent (only the standard rate of tax applies as Gerry's salary does not exceed the standard rate cut-off point).

Then we must deduct Gerry's personal tax credit (€1,650) and also his PAYE credit (€1,650) from his tax liability (€6,500).

6,500 - 1,650 - 1,650 = 2,200

€2,200 is the actual tax liability that Gerry is liable to pay on his yearly salary of €32,500. Note: this figure of €2,200 can be further reduced.

EXAMPLE 2

Thomas is a single man who earns €47,000 per year. This is like the previous example except that Thomas exceeds the standard cut-off point and he must pay a percentage of his salary at both the standard rate and the higher rate. In this case, we must calculate Thomas's tax liability up to the standard rate and the remainder of his salary must be calculated at the higher rate. We will now see how this is done.

47,000 (salary) - 32,800 (standard rate cut-off point) = 14,200 (this figure is taxable at the higher rate)
Standard rate calculation: 32,800 x 0.20 = 6,560
Higher rate calculation: 14,200 x 0.41 = 5,822

We then add the liability at the standard rate and the higher rate to get the overall liability.

6,560 + 5,822 = 12,382 (this is the tax liability for Thomas per annum)

We then apply Thomas's tax reliefs:

11,710 - 3,300 = 9,082

In cases where the single person qualifies for an allowance for a dependent child, we use the relevant tax band and apply the relevant cut-off points.

EXAMPLE 3
Michael is a married man with three children and earns €67,000 per year. His wife stays at home to mind the children. Michael is the assessable spouse and the couple are assessed jointly. Calculate the tax liability at the standard rate:

67,000 (salary) - 41,800 (standard rate cut-off point) = 25,200 (taxable at the higher rate)

41,800 x 0.20 = 8,360 (tax liability up to standard rate cut-off point)

25,200 x 0.41 = 10,332 (tax liability at the higher rate)

8,360 + 10,332 = 18,692 (total tax liability)

We then apply the tax credits: joint assessment credit + PAYE credit:

3,300 + 1,650 = 4,950

Tax liability - tax credits:
18,692 - 4,950 = 13,742 (this is the figure for Michael's total tax liability)

In all of the examples above, the final figure for each person's tax liability is the figure which applies before any deductions are made for pension contributions or personal reliefs. Over the following chapters, I will show you how to reduce this figure. All the different types of reliefs and ways to reduce this tax liability will be explained. We will return to the examples above and show exactly how these reliefs are applied and how we can reduce the figure for tax liability.

Pension Contributions

As we have seen from the formulae we have used to calculate our tax liability and the practical examples, the figure we ended up with as a tax liability is not a true figure. At this point, it is important to note that payments into private pensions, PRSAs, AVCs and the like are tax deductible from a person's gross pay. Pensions are a great way of both protecting your future when you retire and also of reducing your tax liability. A person may subtract the annual contribution they make to their pension from their gross pay/salary before applying tax rates and bands. This reduces a person's gross pay and reduces the tax liability. The following formula must be introduced before any other calculations are completed:

Salary - Pension contribution = New figure for salary

Having completed this calculation, apply the formulae previously used for calculating tax liability at the standard rate or higher rate – whichever applies. Use the new figure as the salary figure.

Income Levy: 2009

At the start of 2009, a new income levy was introduced on all pay. Originally, the rate was set to apply from 1 January 2009. In the mini-budget announced in early 2009, this figure was adjusted on 1 May 2009. This new Income Levy is payable on gross income from all sources before any tax reliefs, capital allowances, losses, pension contributions or PRSI deductions. To calculate what you pay, use the rates below, relative to your income. Once calculated, the amount of levy payable is deducted from your pay like all other relevant deductions. The rates of the Income Levy which applied from 1 January 2009 up to 30 April 2009 are as follows:

- 1 percent: Income up to €100,100 per annum
- 2 percent: Income between €100,101 and €250,120 per annum
- 3 percent: Income in excess of €250,120 per annum

The rates of the Income Levy which apply from 1 May 2009 and are projected up to and including 31 December 2010 are as follows:

- 2 percent: Income up to €75,036 per annum
- 4 percent: Income between €75,037 and €174,980 per annum
- 6 percent: Income in excess of €174,980 per annum

As the income levy rates and bands were changed during 2009, the following rates of income levy apply for the period 1 January 2009 to 31 December 2009:

- 1.67 percent: Income up to €75,036
- 3 percent: Income between €75,037 and €100,100
- 3.33 percent: Income between €100,101 and €174,980
- 4.67 percent: Income between €174,981 and €250,120
- 5 percent: Income in excess of €250,120

Exempt categories

The income levy does not apply:

- where an individual's income for a year does not exceed €15,028 per annum
- for over-sixty-fives, where their annual income does not exceed €20,000 per annum for a single individual or €40,000 per annum for a married couple
- for holders of full medical cards
- to social welfare payments

Depending on your income amount, just multiply it by the relevant percent for the levy band to which your income applies. In essence, the levy is double taxation, as the amount you pay *is not* deducted from your salary in respect of any tax liability. It is another tax calculated on your basic pay. (A bit unfair, perhaps, but easy for the government to apply and collect.) The formula for calculating your income levy is:

Salary / 100 x levy percentage = levy payable

Note: Many people are paid in arrears or have allowances paid in a specific week of the month. When the levy was introduced on 1 January 2009, it did not take into account any money which, although paid to employees in 2009, was earned in 2008. Thus the levy was wrongly paid against income earned in 2008, when the levy was not in existence. The levy should not have been charged against this income, and a refund of this money may be applied for. This is again the case for when the bands were changed in May 2009. Check your P60 for 2009 to see if you were wrongly charged for this levy. This will probably be the case each time the levy changes!

Universal Social Charge

The Income Levy and the Health Levy were abolished with effect from 1 January 2011 and replaced by the Universal Social Charge (USC). The USC is a tax payable on gross income, including benefits from your employer, but before any deductions for pension contributions. Employers will deduct the USC from payments they make to their employees on a pay-period by pay-period basis.

The rates and thresholds of the USC are as follows:

USC Thresholds	Rate
Individual aged under 70 years:	
Income up to €10,036	2%
Income from €10,036.01 to €16,016	4%
Income above €16,016	7%
Individual aged 70 years or over:	
Income up to €10,036	2%
Income above €10,036	4%

Where an individual's total income for a year does not exceed €4,004, their income will be exempt from the USC. All payments made by the Department of Social Protection, and income already subjected to DIRT, will be exempt from the USC.

New USC Certificate

This is the certificate your employer will give you (with your P45) when you leave your job during the year. This certificate is your personal record of your USC deductions while in employment. You should retain it carefully. It is not necessary to send this certificate to Revenue or give it to your new employer.

Redundancy Rebates

Unfortunately, unemployment has become an all-too-familiar aspect of life, particularly over the last three years. In circumstances where a person is made redundant during the course of the year, it is most likely that they will have paid tax exceeding that for which they are liable. This is most likely in cases where a person's salary exceeds the standard rate cut-off point which applies to them, or if they work for only part of the year.

Tax credits are calculated over a yearly basis and a person's tax credits are divided over fifty-two weeks. Therefore, if a person works for the first thirty-two weeks of the year and is redundant for the rest of the year - twenty weeks - they will have twenty weeks of tax credits to claim back against the tax that they have already paid. If during the weeks of your employment you did not pay any tax, however, you will not be entitled to any refund. The same will apply when a person retires during the year. They should contact their local Revenue office and submit their details.

If I do qualify for a tax refund, how much tax is refunded?

If it is the case that you are entitled to a tax refund, the amount of the refund will depend on:

- The length of time that you are unemployed
- The amount of tax that you have paid since 1 January that year
- The amount of any tax credits which you may have used during the part of the year in which you were working

When can I apply for a refund?

It is not necessary to wait until the end of the year to apply for a refund. In general, you should wait a minimum of four weeks after becoming unemployed before applying for a tax refund. If, however, it is the case that you are in receipt of any other taxable sources of income (for example, social welfare or similar payments from the Department of Social, Community and Family Affairs), you should wait a minimum of eight weeks, as any tax credit will be utilised in part or in full against the other income. In cases where you may have been subject to emergency tax by your employer prior to being made redundant, you may apply *immediately* for a refund.

How do I apply for a refund?

To apply for a refund, you must complete a P50 form and supply it, along with parts 2 and 3 of your P45, given to you by your employer. These documents are then forwarded to your local tax office. Your local tax office will then contact you with the details of any repayment, and a cheque for the amount will be forwarded to you in due course.

In cases where a person is in receipt of Job Seeker's Allowance, which is a taxable source of income, any child-dependent element is exempt from the first €12.70. If you are in receipt of Job Seeker's Allowance and you make a claim for a refund, the taxable part of the allowance will be added to your pay; the appropriate refund, if any, will be made from this new figure. If, however, the weekly amount of your Job Seeker's Benefit exceeds your weekly tax credit, you will not be entitled to any refund.

Emergency Tax

A person who starts in a new job during the course of the year will be liable to Emergency Tax until the tax office can assess what tax should be paid and have the correct details relating to the new employee. The Emergency Basis must be used by an employer when:

- The employer has not received, in respect of the employee, either a Certificate of Tax Credits and Standard Rate Cut-Off Point or a Tax Deduction Card for the current year, or a P45 form for the current year or the previous year
- The employee has given the employer a completed P45 form indicating that the emergency basis applies
- The employee has given the employer a completed P45 without a PPS number and not indicating that the Emergency Basis applies

Tax is calculated on the gross pay (after deduction of pension contributions and permanent health contributions, where relevant). There are different rules which apply, depending on whether or not the employee provides an employer with his or her PPS Number.

No PPS number provided

In circumstances where no PPS number has been provided by a new employee, the employer is obliged to calculate the tax due on the employee's earnings at the higher rate with no tax credit. Where the employee subsequently provides their PPS number, the normal Emergency Basis will apply to his/her earnings from then on.

Validation of PPS number

In the case where a new employee provides an employer with a PPS number, the employer is obliged to take reasonable steps to ensure that the PPS number provided does in fact refer to that employee. The employer will be regarded as having taken reasonable measures if he/she checks the PPS number provided against any of the following documents:

- a tax credit certificate from a previous employment
- a P45 form
- a Social Welfare Services Card or PPSN registration letter issued by the Department of Social and Family Affairs
- Notice of Assessment to Income Tax or Capital Gains Tax
- P21 Balancing Statement form
- P60 form
- any other item of correspondence from Revenue which specifically quotes the PPS number
- a payslip from a previous employer which shows the PPS number.

Normal Emergency rules

Under the normal Emergency Basis where a valid PPS number has been provided, a tax credit and standard rate cut-off point is given for the first number of weeks. These figures are based on the single personal tax credit and standard rate cut-off point for the relevant tax year, regardless of the employee's marital status. The tax deductions are increased progressively after four weeks as follows:

The normal emergency rules where a valid PPS number has been provided			
Weeks of Employment	**Tax Credit**	**Standard Rate Cut-off Point (SCROP)**	**Tax Rate**
Weeks 1 to 4	1/52 of single personal tax credit	1/52 single personal SRCOP	Lowest Rate of Tax
Weeks 5 to 8	Nil tax credit	1/52 single personal SRCOP	Lowest Rate of Tax
Week 9 onwards	Nil tax credit	Nil SRCOP	Highest Rate of Tax

P60

With respect to this book, this is one of the most important documents that you will need in any given year. Every year, usually within the first six weeks from the start of the year, a person who was employed at any stage in the previous year will be issued with a P60 form. This form sets out the earnings of that person for the previous year, along with the tax paid. It will also show the tax credits that were available to the person for that year.

Section A of the P60 relates to a person's gross pay. The figure for this total pay should be the figure that the person earned in the previous year, less any contributions for pensions allowable for income tax purposes. Section B sets out the tax that was paid on a person's gross pay. Also on the P60 will be the figure for the person's yearly tax credit.

To calculate if the tax you paid is correct, use the formulae in the section on tax bands and input the figures from your P60 where applicable. If you have only worked for part of the year and discover that you have paid too much tax, you can claim this back by contacting your local tax office and supplying them with the information they require.

PRSI

As well as PAYE, another form of taxation is Pay Related Social Insurance (PRSI). Employees earning in excess of a particular amount per week are required to pay PRSI. Employers are also obliged to pay on behalf of their employees. There are different rates for both employees and employers, and also for those who are self-employed. In Budget 2010, rates of PRSI figures were left as they were for 2009. As already stated, PRSI will undergo a radical change in 2011 as a new social levy is introduced that incorporates PRSI, health levies and income levies. A review of your payments is very worthwhile and, when contacting your local Revenue office, also give them the figures for PRSI contributions.

The most common rate of PRSI is 4% which is payable by employees and by the self-employed. In general, all employees (whether full-time or part-time) and self-employed workers with an income of €3,174 or more a year (from all sources), who are aged between 16 and 66 years of ages must pay PRSI contributions.

Most employees in Ireland pay Class A PRSI.

PAYE Workers – Class A

- Where an employee earns less than €356 per week, they will be exempt from PRSI.
- Where an employee earns between €356 and €500 per week, they are exempt on the first €127 and are liable to PRSI at 4% on the balance.
- Where an employee earns more than €500 per week, they are liable to PRSI at 4% on the first 127, 8% on income greater than €127 and €1,443 and 9% on income earned over €1,443.

Self Employed persons pay PRSI under Class S

Self-Employed Persons – Class S

- Where weekly income earned does not exceed €500, PRSI is payable on all income at 4%.
- Where weekly income earned exceeds €500, PRSI is payable at 7% on the first €1,443 and at 8% at any income earned in excess of €1,443.
- For Self Employed Persons, the minimum contribution per annum is €253.

Know Your Payslip

Whether you get paid by the week or paid by the month, your employer is obliged by law to supply you with a payslip. It is a good idea to keep all your payslips if you can, particularly the last payslip of the year (week fifty-two pay order). This week fifty-two payslip will give you the totals for all additions and deductions for the year.

The purpose of the payslip is to show you what you are being paid and what deductions are being taken from your gross pay. By learning to read your payslip you will be able to insure that you are being paid properly for the number of hours that you work, that you are receiving the correct tax credit and that your employer is paying the correct PRSI rate for you. Payslips will vary from person to person but the majority of details contained on it will be the same. Below is a sample payslip and underneath is an explanation of each section:

Employee no.	Date	Pay Period	Taxable Pay	Taxable Pay (cum)	Net Amount
23433	2/11	Week 45	977.62	42899.39	653.23
Tax Credit	Tax Credit (cum)	Cut Off Point	Cut Off Point (cum)	Tax	Tax (cum)
106.92	476.92	873.08	34923.08	63.60	5977.98
Additions	Hours	This P.O.	Deductions	This P.O.	Total This Year
Salary overtime	 5.25	887.00 90.62	PRSA pension Income levy PRSI PAYE VHI SIPTU Fees	125.00 19.55 68.04 63.60 42.00 6.20	5625.00 857.98 3025.55 5977.98 1680.00 248.00

EMPLOYEE NUMBER

This is your unique employee number which you will receive from your employer. You will be able to reference this number in relation to internal queries.

DATE

This is the date on which your wages will be paid or transferred into your bank account.

PAY PERIOD

This indicates which week of the year the pay relates to.

TAXABLE PAY

This is the gross figure for your pay which includes your basic salary, overtime and taxable allowances. It does not include non-taxable allowances.

TAXABLE PAY (CUMULATIVE)
This is the figure for taxable pay for the year to date.

NET AMOUNT
This is the figure that you will receive as your pay after all taxes and deductions are paid. It is your take home pay.

TAX CREDIT
The total figure from your certificate of tax credits will be divided by fifty-two weeks. This figure will be inserted here, which gives you your weekly tax credit before tax is applied to your taxable pay.

TAX CREDIT (CUMULATIVE)
This is the figure for tax credits granted apportioned for the year to date.

CUT-OFF POINT
This shows the point to which the standard rate applies. Any figure above this is subject to the higher rate of tax.

CUT-OFF POINT (CUMULATIVE)
This is the figure to date of weekly cumulative cut-off points.

TAX
This is the tax that you paid for this pay period.

TAX (CUMULATIVE)
This is the tax that you have paid to date for that year.

ADDITIONS
In this column you will ordinarily find totals for your basic pay, overtime payable, taxable allowances and non-taxable allowances.

HOUR
This will contain the number of hours payable for each addition.

THIS P.O.
P.O. stands for Pay Order. This gives the monetary totals for each addition.

DEDUCTIONS
All deductions from your pay should be listed in this column. You would normally expect to find deductions for tax, PRSI, pension contributions, income levy and any other deductions authorised by you.

THIS P.O.
This contains the totals for all deductions.

TOTAL THIS YEAR
This column lists the total deductions for the year to date.

3

Other Tax Reliefs

There are a range of other tax reliefs which a person may qualify for. These are listed and explained below. If any of these credits relate to you, they can be claimed through your local Revenue office. Many of these reliefs can be claimed retrospectively, so take the time to ensure that you review your circumstances in previous years as well as in the current year, as you may qualify for previous years. Some reliefs are claimed in the year following qualification, and others can be claimed in the year for which they apply. Relief can come in the form of rebates on your wages, increases in your personal tax reliefs or cheques issued to you personally. Each part will be broken down, explaining what the relief is, to whom it applies, the qualifying criteria, the amount of relief, and how to apply. Add this figure to the relief calculator on page 125 to calculate your total relief and the amount of tax that should be paid.

Widowed Person's Credit

What is the widowed person's credit and to whom is it available?

The widowed person's credit is available to widowed persons who have one or more dependent children and satisfy the following criteria:

- The widowed person must not have remarried before the start of the tax year
- The qualifying child must be resident with the individual for all or part of the tax year
- The tax credit is not due to a person who is living with another person as husband and wife.

Only one tax credit is granted, irrespective of the number of children and it is not due in the year of bereavement. Widowed person's relief is broken up into a number of different categories, and the amount of relief due replaces that provided by a person's personal tax relief.

Widowed Person's Relief (showing relief due in euro)						
Widowed Person	**2011**	**2010**	**2009**	**2008**	**2007**	**2006**
(Other years) with dependent children	1,650	1,830	1,830	1,830	1,760	1,630
(Other years) Without dependent children	2,190	2,430	2,430	2,430	2,310	2,130
Bereavement year – without dependent children	3,660	3,660	3,660	3,660	3,520	3,260
Widowed Parent – 1st year after death	3,600	4,000	4,000	4,000	3,750	3,100
Widowed Parent – 2nd year after death	3,150	3,500	3,500	3,500	3,250	2,600
Widowed Parent – 3rd year after death	2,700	3,000	3,000	3,000	2,750	2,100
Widowed Parent – 4th year after death	2,250	2,500	2,500	2,500	2,250	1,600
Widowed Parent – 5th year after death	1,800	2,000	2,000	2,000	1,750	1,100

How do I claim the relief due to me?

A person who can claim widowed person's relief may do so by contacting their local Revenue office with their PPS number. You may be asked for other documentation, such as a copy of a death certificate.

Home Carer's Relief

What is Home Carer's Relief and to whom is it available?

Home Carer's Relief is a relief available where a person cares for the well-being of a qualifying child or elderly person. It is only available to persons who are married and are assessed jointly. The tax credit is not available to married couples who are taxed as single persons. Neither is it available to married couples with combined incomes of over €41,800 in the tax year 2011 or €45,400 in 2009 and 2010, and who claim the increased standard rate tax band for dual-income couples. Taxpayers should decide whether it would be more beneficial to increase the standard rate tax band by the income of the carer or to claim the Home Carers Tax Credit instead.

A dependent person must not be a spouse, and should be: over sixty-five years old; a child in receipt of child benefit or; a person who is permanently incapacitated by reason of mental or physical infirmity. The incapacitated person does not have to reside with the carer. They can live next door or in a neighbouring house, but their residence must be within two kilometres of the carer's residence.

What relief is due?

A tax credit at the standard rate of tax (20 percent) in the tax years 2008 to 2011 is available for married couples where one spouse (the 'home carer') works in the home caring for one or more dependent persons, i.e.: a child for whom they are entitled to Social Welfare child benefit; a person aged sixty-five or over; or a person who is permanently incapacitated by reason of mental or physical infirmity. The qualifying person can either live with those who are caring for them or within two kilometres. The home carer's income should not be in excess of €5,080. A reduced tax credit applies where the income is between €5,080 and €6,880 from 2008 to 2010.

Home Carer's Credits (in euro)						
	2011	**2010**	**2009**	**2008**	**2007**	**2006**
Home Carer's Credit (Max)	810	900	900	900	770	770

The formula

If the carer earns less than €5,080 per annum and the combined income of the couple is less than €45,400 (2010 figure), and the answer to all the above criteria is yes, then you qualify for the full relief allowance of €900. Add this to the total section of the relief calculator on page 125. If the above criteria are met, but the carer earns between €5,080 and €6,880, the relief is due at half the rate relative to a restriction at the cut-off point.

(Earnings < 6,880 – 5,080) / 2 = figure to be subtracted from max relief (€900)

EXAMPLE

Earning = €5,750 (This can be any figure up to €6,880)

5,750 – 5,080 = 670

670 is then divided by 2, as the relief is given at this level at half the rate minus the allowance:

670 / 2 = 335

We then take this figure of 335 from 900, as this is the maximum relief:

900 - 335 = 565

€565 is the amount of relief due in this case.

How do I claim the relief due to me?

A person can claim this relief by completing and submitting Revenue form IT 66 Home Carer's Tax Credit and submitting it to their local tax office.

Age Tax Credit

What is Age Tax Credit and to whom is it available?

People over the age of sixty-five are entitled to a further tax relief depending on whether they are single, widowed or married. The tax credit is doubled for married couples who have opted for joint assessment or separate assessment if either spouse is sixty-five at any time during the tax year. It would be normal that Age Tax Credit would be implemented automatically at the beginning of the year after a person turns sixty-five. It may be the case that a proportion of the credit of the amount allowed may not have been paid in the year that a person has turned sixty-five and thus can be reclaimed.

What relief is due?

Age Tax Credit (in euros)						
	2011	**2010**	**2009**	**2008**	**2007**	**2006**
Single person	245	325	325	325	275	250
Married person	490	650	650	650	550	500

How do I claim the relief due to me?

You can claim this relief by contacting your local tax office with your PPS number. Claims can also be made retrospectively.

Income Tax Exemption and Marginal Relief

Income Tax Exemption and Marginal Relief has been available since 2007 to persons over sixty-five years of age who are single, widowed and married. Before 2007, it was also available to persons under sixty-five. Persons under sixty-five can still claim exemption and Marginal Relief up to 31 December 2007. If you were assessed under the tax credit system and the exemption would be more beneficial, you can ask the Revenue to review your situtation, and you may be due a refund.

A person is exempt from income tax where their total income is less than the following amounts: €18,000 for those aged sixty-five years and over or single/widowed persons, and €36,000 for married persons. These exemption limits are increased by €575 for each of the first two children and by €830 for each subsequent child. A dependent child is a child of the claimant who is:

- under eighteen years of age
- over eighteen years and in full-time education or training full-time as an apprentice, where the training is for at least two years
- incapacitated either physically or mentally, having become so before reaching twenty-one years of age, or after reaching the age of twenty-one but while still in full-time education or while training full-time for a trade or profession for a minimum of two years.

How is exemption granted?

The exemption is granted, and you will not pay any tax, if your total income is less than your relevant exemption limit set out above. A tax credit certificate will be issued to your employer or the payer of your pension showing the exemption figure, so that tax will not be deducted from your salary or pension. *If you have been granted exemption, there will be no additional relief due on any further claims you might have, e.g. health expenses.* The weekly and monthly breakdown of these figures (in euro) is:

Current Figures (in euros)		
	Weekly	**Monthly**
No dependent children	346	1,500
1 dependent child	357	1,548
2 dependent children	368	1,595
3 dependent children	384	1,665

If you are married, it is the older spouse's age that is relevant (For example, if you are sixty-seven and your spouse is sixty-three, you are entitled to the married person's exemption limits).

If you have more than three dependent children, add €15.96 to the weekly figure (or €69.17 to the monthly figure) for each subsequent child.

How do I calculate my total income?

Total income for exemption purposes is your gross income (i.e. before any income tax is deducted) from all sources, less certain deductions, such as expenses, covenanted amounts, and so on. Your income from all sources must be included when claiming income tax exemption (salary, pension, rental income, deposit interest, dividend income, and so on). If married and jointly taxed, your spouse's income is also included. Gross figures (i.e. before deduction of DIRT, Dividend Withholding Tax, and so on) must be included for deposit interest and dividend income. If your total income is equal to or less than the exemption limit, you are exempt from income tax.

EXAMPLE

A married couple (both over sixty-five) have an income of €35,000 in 2010. They will be exempt from tax for 2010 because their gross income of €35,000 is less than the exemption limit of €36,000. Note: Exemption applies to income tax only. PRSI and the Universal Social Charge continue to be payable.

Marginal Relief

If my income is slightly above the exemption limit, do I get any relief?

Yes. If your total income is over the exemption limit that applies to you, you may still qualify for some relief. This is called Marginal Relief and will only be given where it is more beneficial to you than your tax credits. If you have been given marginal relief and subsequently wish to claim any additional tax credits or reliefs (e.g. service charges or health expenses), Revenue will recalculate your liability to examine which is more beneficial to you – tax credits or Marginal Relief. The Marginal Relief tax rate is 40 percent.

How does Marginal Relief work?

The following example shows how Marginal Relief works:

A married man, aged sixty-eight years, with two dependent children, has an income of €40,000 in 2011. He is entitled to a total tax credit of €€5,440, which is made up of: Married Personal Credit €3,300; Age Credit, €490; PAYE Credit, €1,650. The exemption limit that applies to him is €37,150 (€36,000 + €575 + €575 for his two dependent children).

TAXED UNDER NORMAL SYSTEM (20 PERCENT)
Total income: €40,000
Tax @ 20 percent (€8,000), less tax credits of €5,440
Tax liability: €2,560

TAXED UNDER MARGINAL RELIEF (40 PERCENT)
Total income: €40,000
Less exemption of €37,150 (excess of €2,850)
Of this €2,850 he is liable to pay tax at the higher rate of 40 percent
Therefore tax liability: €1,140

In this example, it is more favourable to be granted Marginal Relief, as the tax due is less than that which arises using the tax credits. Once Marginal Relief has been allowed, you and your employer/pension provider should receive a tax credit certificate which will show that you have been granted the relief.

Can I claim a refund of income tax deducted?

If you are entitled to exemption from income tax but have actually paid tax or received income from which tax was deducted (e.g. salary, pension, deposit interest, Irish dividends, income under a covenant, and so on), you will be entitled to a refund in most cases. All claims must be made within a four-year time limit.

How can I claim exemption or Marginal Relief?

If you were granted exemption last year, there is no need to reapply. Exemption will be automatically granted this year, if due. If you think you are entitled to the Income Tax

Exemption or Marginal Relief, you can contact your local Revenue office. See page 132 for the full list of local offices.

Employment Support – Family Income Supplement (FIS)
FIS is a weekly tax-free payment, paid by the Department of Social and Family Affairs, to help your family if your income falls below a certain limit (One-parent families can also qualify). To qualify for this, you must work a minimum of nineteen hours per week (or thirty-eight hours per fortnight) and have at least one dependent child. For further information and application forms, contact your local Social Welfare office.

Tax Relief on DIRT

Am I exempt from Deposit Interest Retention Tax (DIRT)?

You can apply directly to your financial institution to have the interest paid without deduction of DIRT if you or your spouse are aged sixty-five or over during the tax year, or are permanently incapacitated by physical or mental infirmity from maintaining yourself, or if you or your spouse's total income for the year will be below the relevant annual exemption limit.

Tax Relief for Tuition Fees

What is this relief and to whom is it available?

Relief is available to persons who pay tuition fees while attending a third-level college or approved college or while attending an approved course. Up to 2006, inclusive, an individual could claim tax relief on fees paid in respect of third-level courses on his/her own behalf or on behalf of a spouse, child or person for whom the individual is or was the legal guardian. With effect from 2007, the required relationship has been abolished and an individual can claim tax relief on fees paid for third-level courses as long as he or she has paid the qualifying fees.

Tax relief at the standard rate of tax is available for tuition fees paid for certain full-time and part-time undergraduate courses of at least two years' duration. The relief applies to fees up to €5,000. Relief is also available for tuition fees paid for certain training courses in the areas of information technology and foreign languages.

Amount of relief

Relief is available at the standard rate of income tax, and there is a 'cap' on the amount of relief that may be claimed. Relief is *not* available in respect of:

- any part of the tuition fees that are, or will be, met directly or indirectly by grants or scholarships, or by an employer or otherwise
- administration, registration or examination fees.

Relief is available per course, per academic year. Claims for more than one child can be made. The maximum level of relief is €5,000 per course (€3,175 prior to 2005).

If you have paid college fees for more than one individual attending college in an academic year, relief is due to you on the fees paid for each person up to the maximum limit per course. Where fees are paid in instalments, and any such instalments are paid in a tax year following the year in which the academic year of the course commenced, then the relief for fees may be granted either:

- in the tax year during which the academic year of the approved course commenced, or
- in the tax year in which the instalment was paid.

Relief will only be granted, however, in respect of amounts actually paid and subject to the maximum relief available in that academic year.

How may the relief be claimed?

You can apply for this relief by completing the form contained in Revenue leaflet IT 31a. You should retain a receipt provided in relation to tuition fees from the course for which relief has been claimed, as it may be requested for verification at a later date. Relief shall not be given in respect of a year of assessment for more than one approved course per student. However, as stated earlier, the person paying the fees can claim relief if they pay for a multiple of courses. The following documentation is required with each claim:

- amount of tuition fees
- name and address of individual who paid tuition fees
- name and address of student
- course of study and duration
- confirmation of how the college is funded (publicly or privately) and where it is located (whether in an EU or a non-EU country).

Third-level education

APPROVED COLLEGES

Approved colleges for the purpose of the tuition fees tax relief include:

- universities, public and private colleges, and institutes of higher education in the State that provide courses that are approved for higher education grants
- a college or institution of higher education in the State which operates in accordance with certain codes of standards laid down by the Minister for Education and Science (these colleges and institutions must be approved by the Department of Education and Science for the purposes of this tax relief)
- publicly funded or duly accredited universities and institutions of higher education in another EU member state

- a college or institution of higher education in any other EU Member State providing distance education in this state, which provides courses approved for the Higher Education Grants Scheme (this includes the Open University)
- publicly funded or duly accredited universities and institutions of higher education in non-EU Member States (note: this applies to postgraduate courses only)
- colleges or institutions (in the State or in any other EU Member State) which provide distance education in the State and which operate in accordance with a certain code of standards laid down by the Minister for Education and Science (these colleges and institutions must be approved by the Department of Education and Science).

Approved undergraduate courses

Undergraduate courses must be:

- carried out in an approved college
- of at least two academic years' duration, and
- approved by the Department of Education and Science.

Approved postgraduate courses

Postgraduate courses must:

- be carried out in an approved college
- be of at least one but no more than four academic years in duration, and
- lead to a postgraduate award based on either a thesis or an examination.

Also, the person taking the course must already have a primary degree or equivalent qualification.

Contact your local Revenue office to see if the course is approved.

Foreign-language and FÁS courses:
This relief is allowable per course per academic year, with a minimum relief of €315 and maximum of €1,270 per course.

Relief for Blind Persons and Guide Dogs

What is this relief and to whom is it available?

A person who is blind at any time during the tax year may claim this relief. Where a couple are married and both are blind, the tax credit is doubled. Children who are regarded as blind do not qualify for this allowance. In cases of this nature, incapacitated child tax credit may be claimed. Relief is granted to the above persons in cases where their vision is impaired to the extent that:

- the central visual acuity does not exceed 6/60 in the better eye with corrective lenses, or
- the widest diameter of the visual field subtends an angle no greater than 20 percent.

What relief is available?

The relief available is:

	2011	2010	2009	2008	2007	2006
Blind person, one spouse blind	1,650	€1,830	€1,830	€1,830	€1,760	€1,500
Blind person, both spouses blind	3,300	€3,660	€3,660	€3,660	€3,520	€3,000

How can this relief be claimed?

To make a claim, a person must complete the form for Blind Persons Tax Credit & Guide Dog Allowance contained in Revenue leaflet IT 35 to their local tax office, along with their PPS Number. The claimant must have in their possession a letter from an ophthalmic surgeon stating their level of blindness and whether their blindness is temporary or permanent. A certificate from an optician or doctor will not suffice.

What reliefs are available for people with guide dogs?

In cases where a blind person maintains a trained guide dog and is in receipt of a letter from the Irish Guide Dog Association confirming registered ownership of the dog, they may also qualify for relief. It is not necessary to submit this letter but it must be retained for a period of six years, as the claim may be subject to an audit at some point.

What relief is due?

Relief in respect of a guide dog is available at the standard rate of tax, up to a maximum of €825. Up to the end of 2008, relief was available at the marginal rate of tax.

VAT exemptions on equipment

A blind person is entitled to claim repayment of Irish VAT paid on the purchase or importation of aids and appliances designed to help a blind person in their day-to-day functions (e.g. specially adapted computer equipment, Braille books, Braille writing equipment, and so on).

Dependent Relative Relief

Dependent Relative Relief is available to persons who maintain at their own expense a relative who is incapacitated by old age or infirmity from maintaining him/herself, or is a widowed mother/mother-in-law or widowed father/father-in-law, regardless of age and state of health, and whose income does not exceed the specified amount. For 2001 onwards, the specified amount is calculated as follows:

Maximum of the Old Age Contributory Pension (over-eighty) + Living Alone Allowance + the Island Allowance + €280

The Dependent Relative Tax Credit can also be claimed by an individual who maintains, at their own expense, a son or daughter who resides with them and on whose services they depend due to old age or infirmity.

Who can claim the relief?

This relief is available to a person who maintains a dependent relative at their own expense. If more than two people contribute to the maintenance of the relative, the relief is shared appropriate to their contribution. The relative being cared for must be either widowed, of old age, infirm, or on low income.

How is the relief claimed?

The relief may be claimed through a person's local Revenue office, using form IT 46.

What are the rates of relief?

In 2005, the rate of relief was €60. From 2006 to 2010, the rate of relief available was €80 and in 2011, the relief available is €70. There is also a limit on earnings for the qualifying recipient as follows:

2011	2010	2009	2008	2007	2006	2005
€3,660	€3,660	€3,660	€3,660	€3,000	€1,500	€1,000

Incapacitated Child Relief

Who can claim?

A parent or a legal guardian may claim the relief where that parent or guardian maintains an incapacitated child. The child must have become physically or mentally incapacitated before they have turned twenty-one or, if after twenty-one, while in full-time education or learning a trade.

For this section, 'child' includes: a stepchild; a formally adopted child; or an informally adopted child or any child of whom the claimant has custody and whom he/she maintains at his/her own expense.

If the incapacity can be corrected, treated or relieved by the use of any treatment, device, medication or therapy, the child is not regarded as permanently incapacitated. Examples are diabetes which can be treated with insulin, coeliac diseases, hearing impairment which can be corrected by hearing aid, and so on.

Where more than one child is incapacitated, a tax credit may be claimed for each child. *If a child does not satisfy all the conditions for the tax credit, the claimant may claim Dependent Relative Tax Credit.*

How do I claim this relief?

A claim may be made by a qualifying person by contacting their local tax office and providing them with the following information:

- Name of Child
- Birth Certificate of Child

- Nature of the incapacity (a doctor's certificate may also be required)

Rate of relief

The rates of relief from 2005 to the present are as follows:

	2011	2010	2009	2008	2007	2006
One Parent Family - Single	€3,300	€1,830	€1,830	€1,830	€1,760	€1,630
One Parent Family - Widowed	€3,300	€1,830	€1,830	€1,830	€1,760	€1,630

Relief in cases where a person is employed to care for an incapacitated person

Who can claim?

A family member who employs a person to care for an incapacitated relative who fulfils the criteria listed below can claim this relief.

What are the qualifying conditions?

The individual must be completely incapacitated by physical or mental infirmity. Incapacity must be throughout the year of assessment. However, it is not necessary for the person to be employed for the full year. While the words 'throughout the year of assessment' prohibit the claiming of the relief for the year during which the individual became completely incapacitated, with effect from 1 January 2004, relief may be allowed for that year also. The carer may be employed through an agency.

How much relief is due?

The amount of the allowance is the net cost of employing the person (i.e. the cost of employing the person less any amount received from the Health Service Executive, local authority, and so on), subject to a maximum limit. It is not conditional on the claimant to register as an employer but, as an employer, they will have certain PAYE/PRSI obligations. Claims are processed through the person's local tax office by completing Form HKL. The tax relief is available on the cost of employing the carer up to a maximum of €50,000. The relief is allowed in the form of a deduction from gross income. If two or more persons are entitled to claim this deduction in respect of the same incapacitated individual, then the relief is apportioned between the two in proportion to the amount of the employment cost they have borne and the total shall not exceed €50,000.

One Parent Family Tax Relief

What is One Parent Family Tax Relief and who can claim it?

This relief is available to an individual (whether widowed, single, divorced, deserted or separated) who has a dependent child resident with him/her overnight for all or part of the tax year. To qualify for the relief, a person must not be entitled to the Married Personal Tax Credit and also must not be living with another person as husband and wife.

What relief is due, and how do I claim?

The rates of relief are shown in the table below:
To make a claim for One Parent Family Relief, a qualifying person must complete and submit Form OP 1 to their local Revenue office. (See list of offices on page 132.)

Anything else I need to know?

The tax credit is fixed, irrespective of the number of children. The tax credit is not apportioned between claimants. Each parent receives the full tax credit once the child resides with both parents for at least part of the relevant tax year.

The term 'child' includes a stepchild, an informally adopted child or any child the claimant has custody of and maintains at his/her expense. The term 'dependent child' refers to a child under eighteen years of age, or over eighteen if in full-time education or permanently incapacitated.

4

Work-related Reliefs

Trade Union Subscription Relief

What is Trade Union Subscription Relief and to whom is it available?

If you are, or ever have been, a member of a trade union, chances are that you are entitled to tax relief at the standard rate of 20 percent of fees paid, to a maximum of €70. Relief is available to any person who is a member of a trade union at any time during the year of assessment. The trade union must be:

- the holder of a negotiation licence under the Trade Union Act 1941
- an exempted body within the meaning of Section 6 of the Trade Union Act 1941, as amended by the Trade Union Act 1942
- a Garda Representative Body, or
- a Defence Forces Representative Body.

Relief due

The figures on the following page are the maximum rates of relief due over the last five years. Retrospective claims may be made once all details have been supplied. This relief is being abolished for 2011 and subsequent years.

Trade Union Subscription Relief rates				
2010	2009	2008	2007	2006
€70	€70	€70	€60	€60

How do I claim the relief?

You can claim your relief for trade union subscriptions by contacting your local Revenue office and supplying the relevant details.

Childcare Services Relief

What is this relief and to whom is it available?

Childcare Service Relief is available when a person minds children for payment. If a person minds up to three children in the home of the carer, and if the earnings are less than €15,000 per annum, then they are exempt from tax. If they earn more than €15,000, normal tax rates and bands apply.

Revenue Job Assist

What is this relief and to whom is it available?

Additional tax relief at the individual's highest rate of tax (i.e. 20 percent or 41 percent from 2008 to 2011), is available for people who have been unemployed for one year or more and who take up a qualifying job. Relief in the first year of employment is €3,810 plus €1,270 for each child, reducing to two-thirds of that amount in year two and one-third in year three. This relief is also available for people who have been in receipt of Disability Allowance, Blind Person's Pension or Invalidity Pension for twelve months or more; who have been in receipt of Illness Benefit for three years or more; or who have been released after twelve months or more in prison.

What are the criteria for qualifying?

The claimant must take up an employment which:

- starts on or after 6 April 1998
- is for a minimum period of thirty hours per week
- is capable of lasting twelve months

and where:

- the previous holder was not unfairly dismissed
- the employment is not primarily commissioned-based (i.e. over 75 percent of earnings derived from commission)
- there were no redundancies in the company in the previous twenty-six weeks
- it is not an employment where the employer requires no workforce

Revenue Job Assist only applies if you are taking up a job. It does not apply if you are becoming self-employed. The scheme also applies to people who were involved in the following, provided they were in receipt of one of the payments listed previously immediately prior to commencing the course or scheme:

- certain FÁS training courses (non-apprenticeship)
- the Community Employment Scheme
- the Job Initiative programme
- the 'Workplace' five-week job experience programme
- the Back to Education scheme administered by the Department of Social and Family Affairs

What if I was in prison?

Time spent in prison will count as a period of unemployment for Revenue Job Assist if you fall into one of the following categories:

- with effect from 31 July 1998, prisoners released under the terms of the Good Friday Agreement can qualify for this relief provided the period spent in prison was for a continuous period of at least twelve months immediately prior to the date you started this job
- with effect from 1 January 2006, if you have been released from prison, periods spent in prison are deemed equivalent to periods of unemployment

Additional tax allowances

The additional tax allowances are an Extra Personal Tax Allowance and a Child Tax Allowance for each qualifying child. These allowances are marginally rated (which means that they are allowed at the individual's highest rate of tax and appear as an increase to your tax credits and standard rate cut-off point on the Tax Credit Certificate). The Revenue Job Assist can be claimed for three years. Also, this tax allowance can be claimed irrespective of your marital status.

What income can I claim the tax allowances against?

The tax allowances can only be set against income from the new job.

When can I claim the tax allowances?

You can start to claim the tax allowances either in the tax year in which you take the job (the tax year runs from 1 January to 31 December), or in the following tax year.

For example, if you took up a job on 1 June 2006, you could start claiming the tax allowances in either the tax year 2006 or 2007. If your income from the new job in the first year is low, it may be more beneficial to wait until the following tax year to start claiming so that you will get the full benefit of the allowances.

Extra Personal Tax Allowance/ Child Tax Allowance		
	First child	**Each subsequent child**
Year 1	€3,810	€1,270
Year 2	€2,540	€850
Year 3	€1,270	€425

How do I qualify for the Extra Child Tax Allowance?

An extra tax allowance can be claimed for each qualifying child. A qualifying child is a child of yours who is:

- under eighteen years of age
- over eighteen years of age and in full-time education or full-time training as an apprentice where the training is for at least two years
- physically or mentally incapacitated, having become so either while in full-time education or while under twenty-one years of age

The child must be resident with you for the whole or part of the tax year.

Can two people claim for the same child?

Yes, but only one allowance can be claimed for each qualifying child in any year. If two people are entitled to claim for the same child, the allowance is split between them as follows:

- where the child is maintained by one person only, that person receives the allowance
- where the child is maintained jointly, the allowance is split either in the same proportion as they each maintain the child or in such manner as they jointly decide.

What happens if I change jobs?

If you change jobs once during the three years, you can keep the allowance. If, however, you move on to a third job, you will lose the allowance. Note: You can only claim this relief for one three-year period. If you claim the relief, become unemployed and then return to work again in the same three-year period, you can continue to claim. If you claim the relief, become unemployed and return to work after the three-year period, you cannot claim the relief.

Can I retain my medical card and secondary benefits?

Under Revenue Job Assist, you can retain your medical card for three years from the date you return to work. You may also retain secondary benefits such as rent/mortgage subsidy, fuel allowance, and so on, for three years, subject to certain income limits and other conditions. For queries in relation to entitlement, or otherwise, to secondary benefits, please contact the Health Service Executive directly.

Can I claim the Family Income Supplement (FIS)?

Yes, you can claim FIS (a weekly tax-free payment) if your family income falls below a certain limit.

How do I make a claim?

Claims are made using the RJA1 form. There are two parts to this form. Part 1 must be completed by you, and Part 2 must be completed by your employer to certify that the job you are taking up qualifies for the scheme. When both parts of the form have been completed, you should forward it to your local Revenue office.

Cycle to Work Scheme

Although not exactly a tax relief, I have decided to include this as it is a very innovative scheme which is of great benefit to both the finances and health of any participants. The scheme is the idea of the Green Party and is aimed at getting people to cycle to work instead of driving their cars. It has been in place since 1 January 2009.

What is the scheme and what equipment can I buy?

The scheme is a tax incentive aimed at encouraging more employees to cycle to and from work. The purpose of the scheme is to exempt from income tax the benefit-in-kind arising from the provision by an employer to an employee or director of a bicycle and safety equipment used mainly for qualifying journeys.

There is a limit of €1,000 on the amount of expenditure an employer can incur in respect of any one employee or director. Additionally, the exemption from income tax in respect of the benefit-in-kind can only be availed of once in any five-year period by an employee or director.

As stated earlier, the bicycle provided must be used for what is termed a 'qualifying journey'. This means the whole or part (e.g. between home and train station) of the journey between the employee's or director's home and normal place of work, or between his or her normal place of work and another place of work. While an employer will not be required to monitor the use of the bicycle/safety equipment, the employer will be required to obtain a signed statement from the employee or director that the bicycle is for his or her own use and will be used mainly for qualifying journeys.

What bicycles and equipment can I buy?

The exemption will cover pedal bicycles, tricycles and pedelecs (an electrically assisted bicycle which requires some effort on the part of the cyclist in order to effect propulsion). It will not cover motorbikes, scooters or mopeds. The following safety equipment will be covered by the exemption:

- cycle helmets which conform to European standard EN 1078
- bells and bulb horns
- lights, including dynamo packs
- mirrors and mudguards to ensure rider's visibility is not impaired
- cycle clips and dress guards
- panniers, luggage carriers and straps to allow luggage to be safely carried
- locks and chains to ensure cycle can be safely secured
- pumps, puncture repair kits, cycle tool kits and tyre sealant for minor repairs
- reflective clothing, along with white front reflectors and spokes
- reflectors

Who can avail of the scheme and how does it work?

The scheme will only apply where bicycles/safety equipment are made available by the employer generally to all of its directors and employees.

Purchase of bicycles and safety equipment

The employer must purchase the bicycle and safety equipment. The exemption will not apply where an employee or director purchases a bicycle and safety equipment and gets reimbursed by his or her employer.

Salary sacrifice arrangements

An employer and employee may enter into a salary sacrifice arrangement whereby the employee agrees to forego part of his or her salary to cover the costs associated with the purchase of the bicycle and safety equipment. In such circumstances, the employee will not be liable to tax, PRSI or levies on the salary forgone. Where salary sacrifice arrangements are used, they must be completed over a maximum of twelve months from the date of provision of the bicycle and safety equipment. In the specific context of the provision of a bicycle and safety equipment, Revenue will be prepared to regard salary sacrifice arrangements which meet the following conditions as being effective for tax purposes:

- There must be a bona fide and enforceable alteration to the terms and conditions of employment (exercising a choice of benefit instead of salary)
- The alteration must not be retrospective and must be evidenced in writing
- There must be no entitlement to exchange the benefit for cash
- The choice exercised (i.e. benefit instead of salary) cannot be made more than once in a five-year period
- The choice exercised must be irrevocable for the relevant year for which it is made.

Other points of interest

If an employee wishes to spend more than €1000, they are entitled to do so. However, only the first €1,000 will be exempt from the benefit-in-kind charge to income tax.

If you do not spend the full €1,000 on your bicycle and equipment, you will not be able to claim exemption from the benefit-in-kind charge in respect of the difference between €1,000 and the amount spent by the employer within the five-year period. The exemption is available only once in every five-year period.

The exemption only applies to expenditure on the purchase of a whole bicycle or associated safety equipment.

The rules regarding the €1,000 limit on expenditure and the availability of the exemption once in every five-year period will also apply in the case of bicycle safety equipment.

The bicycle can be bought anywhere, e.g. online from abroad. Employees can choose the bicycle and safety equipment themselves. But It is for employers to decide how they will operate the scheme. Some employers may allow employees to select the bicycle/safety equipment from the retailer of their choice and the employer may then put in place appropriate invoicing and delivery arrangements with the retailer. However, other employers may offer more limited options to employees. An employer could, for example, allow an employee to choose only from the range available from a single retailer.

There will be no threshold on the amount of days a bicycle should be used. However, the bicycle must be used mainly for qualifying journeys.

There will be no notification process involved but the purchase of bicycles and associated safety equipment by employers for directors and employees will be subject to the normal Revenue audit procedure with the normal obligations on employers to maintain records (e.g. delivery dockets, invoices, payments details, salary sacrifice agreements between employer and employee, signed statements from employees that the bicycle/bicycle safety equipment is for own use and will be used for travelling to and from work).

VAT is payable on all bicycles and equipment bought. The employer will not be able to claim an input credit in respect of the VAT payable as the bicycles will not be used for the purposes of taxable supplies.

How do I get my bicycle and what are the financial benefits?

Get your company to sign up for the scheme. Visit your local participating bicycle shop to choose your equipment and obtain a written quote. Return the quotation to your HR scheme administrator to forward to the Bike to Work scheme to request a voucher. Once the voucher is requested, Bike to Work will invoice your employer for the bike package. Complete and sign the purchase agreement (which is sent to you by your company) and return it to your HR person at your participating company. Once payment is made for the bike package by the company, you collect your voucher from them. Redeem your voucher at the bike shop and collect your goods (you must provide your company photo ID card or current driver's license or passport to do this).

What relief is available?

There is tax relief available to both the employer and the employees. Employers receive relief in the form of reduced employer PRSI payments. The relief for employees is based on the rate of taxation that the person pays, whether it be at the standard rate or higher rate. The table below illustrates the savings available at both rates, currently 20 percent (standard) and 41 percent (higher). Public sector workers also receive relief on the pension levy at a rate of another 4 percent.

Employee Expenses

Flat Rate (employment) expenses

These are expenses that are incurred in the performance of the duties of employment and are directly related to the 'nature of the employee's employment'. A standard flat rate expenses allowance (deduction) is set for various classes of employee. For example, airline cabin crews are granted flat rate expenses of €64 per annum. (See Flat Rate Expenses list in Appendix C.) The amount of the deduction is agreed between Revenue and representatives of groups or classes of employees (usually the employees are represented by trade union officials). The agreed deduction is then applied to all employees of the class or group in question.

Round sum expenses

Round sum expenses payments (lump sum expenses payments), whether paid weekly, monthly, yearly or otherwise, which are paid to the employee to cover expenses, must be treated as pay and taxed accordingly. An example of a round sum payment is where an employer agrees to pay say €300 per month in addition to basic salary in order to cover expenses. This €300 must be treated as pay and taxed accordingly.

Meal allowances

Round sum meal expenses payments are taxable in full and must be treated as pay. See above paragraph 'Round-Sum Expenses'.

Meal Vouchers

Where an employer provides luncheon or meal vouchers to employees, there is a taxable benefit and the face value of the vouchers (disregarding 19c per voucher) must be treated as pay and taxed accordingly.

Canteen Meals

A taxable benefit does not arise in respect of free or subsidised meals in staff canteens where meals are provided for the staff generally. The facility must be available to all employees. Otherwise, the exemption does not apply.

Reimbursement of allowable expenses

Payments made to the employee, which are no more than reimbursement of vouched expenses, incurred by the employee in performing the duties of the employment should not be treated as pay. Expenses which are not treated as pay must not only be actually incurred in the performance of the duties of the employment but must also be 'wholly, exclusively and necessarily' so incurred. Expenses which are incurred by employees in travelling to and from the place of employment are not allowable for tax purposes and any reimbursement of these expenses must be treated as pay and taxed accordingly.

Motoring expenses

Some employees use their private cars for business purposes. Reimbursement of motoring expenses incurred can be dealt with in various ways. Remember that round-sum motoring expenses payments are taxable in full and must be treated as pay. See earlier paragraph on 'Round-Sum Expenses'.

Reimbursement of motoring expenses by flat-rate kilometric allowances

Where employees use their private cars for business purposes, reimbursement in respect of allowable motoring expenses can be made by way of flat-rate kilometric allowances. There are two types of kilometric allowance schemes which are acceptable for tax purposes, if an employee bears all the motoring expenses:

- the prevailing schedule of Civil Service rates, or
- any other schedule with rates not greater than the Civil Service rates.

Form IT 51 (Employees' Motoring Expenses) gives full details.

EXPENSES CLAIMS SUBMITTED TO REVENUE

As an alternative to the reimbursement by the employer, an employee may submit a claim to Revenue (Car Expenses claim form) for an expenses deduction (and any wear and tear allowance in respect of the motor vehicle). However, where the employee decides to make such a claim, any reimbursement of expenses by the employer, including any scale allowances, must be treated as pay and taxed accordingly. Employees cannot claim from Revenue for any expenses that are or will be reimbursed by the employer. The following information is required:

- date of purchase of car
- purchase price
- whether new/second-hand
- date from which car was used for business purposes
- mileage and percentage of business to private use
- running costs – repairs, service, tax and insurance
- any reimbursement of running costs made by the employer

Subsistence allowances

Form IT 54 (Employees' Subsistence Expenses) gives full details of subsistence rates for absences within the State, absences outside the State and the rules, etc. in relation to the application of these rates. Remember that round-sum subsistence expenses payments are taxable in full and must be treated as pay (see 'Round-Sum Expenses').

Payments by an employer which do no more than reimburse an employee for allowable subsistence expenses may be made tax-free in certain circumstances. The expenses concerned must have been incurred 'wholly, exclusively and necessarily' in the performance of the duties of the employment.

Where an employee is temporarily away from his/her

normal place of work or is working abroad on a foreign assignment, allowable subsistence expenses can be re-imbursed by the employer on the basis of acceptable flat-rate allowances (Civil Service rates or re-imbursement of subsistence expenses based on any other schedule of rates and related conditions, e.g. country money in the construction industry, which do no more than re-imburse the employee for actual expenditure incurred) or actual expenses which have been vouched with receipts.

5

Housing-related Reliefs

Relief for Service Charges

What is this relief, and to whom does it apply?

Income tax relief is available for individuals who pay local authority and other independent contractors' service charges. These charges include bin charges and charges for water rates. Relief is given for service charges paid in full and on time in the previous calendar year. From 1 January 2012, tax relief will no longer be available on service charges.

Which charges qualify for relief?

- Local authority charges for the provision of domestic water supply, domestic refuse collection or disposal, or domestic sewage disposal
- Group water schemes for domestic water supply
- Independent contractors' charges for domestic refuse collection or disposal.

Who qualifies for relief?

An individual (or his or her spouse, if taxed jointly) who is liable for and pays the service charge on a premises, or an individual (e.g. a son or daughter who lives with an elderly parent) who pays the service charge and lives on a full-time basis in that premises, qualify for this relief.

How much relief is given?

Relief is given at the standard rate. Relief is only granted for the previous year of claim where charges are paid in full and on time. This allowance also applies to the purchase of bin tags. It is not necessary to forward receipts of payment of these charges but receipts should be kept on file by the claimant for production if they are ever requested. Over the years, there have been some adjustments to the relief granted; these are set out below. From 2002 up to and including 2005, reliefs were granted on the full amount paid at the standard rate of 20 percent.

Bin charge / 100 x 20 = rate of relief due

For 2006, the details are as follows: where local authority charges exceeds €400 in 2005, then the full amount of that fixed charge will be allowed. Relief claimed on bin tags purchased in 2005 will be the amount paid in 2005, or €400, whichever is less. Where an individual purchased bin tags and made fixed-charge payments of less than €400 in 2005, a limit of €400 will apply in respect of the total amount paid on both. From 2007 to today, the allowance for both bin charges and tags has been to the limit of €400, allowable at the standard rate of 20 percent. You will receive 20 percent of the fee you pay, up to €400.

Table of reliefs

	2010	2009	2008	2007	2006
Service charges – previous year payment	All incl., max €80	All incl., max €80	All incl., max €80	All incl., max €80	No max

How do I claim the relief?

Claims can be made by submitting the claim form 'Tax Relief for Service Charges Paid' to your local Revenue office.

Rent-a-Room Relief – Rent Tax Credit

Who can claim Rent Tax Credit?

An individual paying for private rented accommodation, used as a sole or main residence, can claim this relief. It includes rent paid for flats, apartments or houses. *This relief is being abolished on a phased basis over the next seven years.* Rent relief can also be claimed where a child is required to pay rent to their parents. The amount paid must be rent as the term would normally be understood, however, and not merely a contribution towards the upkeep of the household. Since 2007, where the Rent Tax Credit is claimed by a child paying rent to his/her parents, the parents will not be allowed to claim the Rent-a-room Relief (allowed to landlords who rent a room out of their principal private residence and whose gross rental income from this does not exceed €10,000, or €7,620 in 2007). This means that the parent will need to declare their rental income on their annual tax return and pay any income tax arising.

How do I claim this relief?

Tax relief may be claimed by a tenant completing a Rent 1 form, which includes their details and those of their landlord. If the landlord lives outside the country, then a claim is made on a R 185 form.

What are the rates of relief?

The rates of relief from 2005 to 2010 are shown on the following page. In cases where the landlord lives outside the country, relief is given at 20 percent and is deducted from the rent payable.

2010	2009	2008	2007	2006
€2,000	€2,000	€2,000	€1,440	€1,320

Relief for rent credit will be withdrawn on a phased basis over the next seven years by reducing the amount of rent that can be relieved at the standard rate of income tax as indicated in the following table:

Tax Year	Single Under 55	Single Over 55	Married/ Widowed Under 55	Married/ Widowed Over 55
2010	2,000	4,000	4,000	8,000
2011	1,600	3,200	3,200	6,400
2012	1,200	2,400	2,400	4,800
2013	1,000	2,000	2,000	3,600
2014	800	1,600	1,600	3,200
2015	600	1,200	1,200	2,400
2016	400	800	800	1,600
2017	200	400	400	800
2018	0	0	0	0

Rent Relief for Private Rented Accommodation

Who can claim this relief?

Where an individual rents a room (or rooms) in a 'qualifying residence' and the gross rent received, including sums arising for food, laundry or similar goods and services, does not exceed €10,000 (or €7,620 in 2007), this income will be exempt from income tax by including it in the individual's tax return. Therefore you as a landlord can earn up to the limit permitted and include it on your tax return and not be liable to pay any tax on this amount. Tax must be paid on any amount which exceeds the limit. There are a number of expenses which can be deducted from the overall figure of rent received if this exceeds €10,000.

What types of rental income are there?

The most common type of rental income comes from letting a house, flat, apartment, office, building or bare land. However, it also includes:

- income from an easement, e.g. if payment is received for the right to erect advertising signs, communication transmitters, or the grant of a right of way or a way-leave
- income arising from the granting of sporting rights, such as fishing and shooting permits
- any payment made by a tenant to defray the cost of work or repairs and maintenance which are not required under the lease agreement to be carried out by the tenant
- certain reverse premiums
- income arising from a conacre letting – the letting of a part of land for just one crop

- service charges in respect of services ancillary to the occupation of property
- insurance recoveries under policies providing cover against non-payment of rent
- premiums and other similar sums received on the grant of certain leases, normally on non-residential property, e.g. a shop or warehouse, that requires the payment of a premium by the tenant to the landlord. Where a lease of less than fifty years is granted, some of the premium charged will be treated as rent.

What expenses can be claimed?

Broadly speaking, you can deduct your rental expenses so long as they are incurred wholly and exclusively for business purposes, and are not of a capital nature. The following are examples of the type of expenses that may be claimed for:

- rents payable by the landlord in respect of the property, e.g. ground rent
- rates or levies payable on the property, i.e. water rates, refuse collection, etc
- cost of any service or goods provided by the landlord, e.g. gas, electricity, central heating, telephone rental, cable television, and so on, for which they do not receive a separate payment
- maintenance, e.g. cleaning and general servicing of the premises
- insurance of the premises against fire, public liability insurance, etc
- management, e.g. the actual cost of the collection of rents, advertising, etc
- legal fees to cover the drawing up of leases or the issue of solicitors' letters to tenants who default on payment of rent

- accountancy fees incurred in preparing a rental income account
- wear and tear on furniture and fittings, e.g. carpets, cookers, central heating, etc
- interest paid on monies borrowed for the purchase, improvement or repair of certain properties
- repairs (which mean 'the restoration of an asset by replacing subsidiary parts of the whole asset', e.g.: exterior/interior painting and decorating, damp and rot treatment, replacing roof slates, mending broken windows, doors, furniture and machines. However, landlords may not claim a deduction for their own labour.)
- certain mortgage protection policy premiums with effect from 1 January 2002
- capital expenditure on certain properties under the various incentive schemes

What about interest paid on borrowings?

Certain restrictions were introduced on the deductibility of interest on borrowed money used on or after 23 April 1998 in the construction, purchase or repair of rented residential premises in the State, or 7 May 1998 in the case of foreign residential premises. However, the relief for interest on borrowed money was restored for such interest accruing on or after 1 January 2002.

There were some transitional arrangements in place in the interim period. Relief is disallowed on interest accruing on or after 6 February 2003 where the let premises was purchased from the spouse of the person who is being charged the rental income. However, the disallowance of interest relief does not apply in the case of legally separated or divorced persons.

Where a loan has been used to purchase, improve or repair a rented residential property and the interest on the loan accrues on or after 7 April 2009, only 75 percent of the interest on the loan can be deducted as a rental expense, instead of the normal 100 percent. For the purposes of the restriction, the interest is treated as accruing on a daily basis. The date the loan is taken out is not relevant.

The restriction does not apply to loans taken out to finance non-residential property and the full amount of interest continues to be deductible in such cases. In the case of mixed residential and non-residential properties, interest should be apportioned on a just and reasonable basis before the restriction is applied to the residential part of the interest.

For the year 2006 onwards interest is not deductible where the person making the claim has not complied with the registration requirements of the Private Residential Tenancies Board in relation to any tenancies in the particular premises. All queries relating to the registration requirements/process should be directed to:

Private Residential Tenancies Board
2nd Floor
O'Connell Bridge House
D'Olier Street
Dublin 2
Telephone: +353 1 635-0600 Monday to Friday
Fax: + 353 1 6350601
www.prtb.ie

Interest on any loan, or part of a loan, that is used to pay stamp duty, legal fees and other expenses incurred in relation to the purchase, improvement or repair of a premises is not deductible. Only interest relating to the actual purchase, improvement or repair costs is deductible.

What expenses can be claimed for wear and tear?

If a furnished premises is let for residential purposes, a claim can be made for a wear-and-tear allowance based on the cost of the furniture and fittings. It will be necessary to retain an itemised list of expenditure incurred each year.

- With effect from 4 December 2002, the allowance is 12.5 percent per year, over eight years.
- For the period between 1 December 2001 and 3 December 2002, the allowance was 20 percent per year, over five years. Transitional provisions apply allowing the rate of 20 percent per year over five years if the item was acquired under a written contract before 4 December 2002 and the expenditure was incurred before 31 January 2003.
- Prior to 1 January 2001, the allowance was 15 percent per year for the first six years and 10 percent in the seventh year.

Relief for refurbishment of certain rented accommodation

Tax relief can be claimed for capital expenditure incurred on or after 6 April 2001 on the refurbishment of rented residential accommodation. The expenditure is allowed as a deduction over a seven-year period: i.e. the expenditure is allowed at a rate of 15 percent per annum for the first six years, with the balance of 10 percent allowed in year seven.

To qualify, the premises must be used as a dwelling and, from the date of completion of the refurbishment, must be let in its entirety under a qualifying lease throughout the relevant period, i.e. ten years from the date of completion of the work or, if later, the date of first letting. A lease is not a qualifying lease if it enables any person to acquire an interest in the premises for a consideration less than the market value. The lessor must comply with the regulations in relation to standards for rented houses, rent books and registration of rented houses.

Where a premises ceases to be a qualifying premises or the lessor passes his or her interest in the premises to another person, the relief will be clawed back in proportion to the amount of time that the premises is let during that year.

Where the lessor passes on his or her interest in the

premises by sale or transfer, then the person who becomes owner of the premises is treated as having incurred the relevant expenditure.

If relief for rental accommodation is given under any other section of the Tax Act, then no relief will be given under this section.

What expenses cannot be claimed for?

- Pre-letting expenses, i.e. expenses incurred prior to the date on which the premises was first let, apart from auctioneer's letting fees, advertising fees and legal expenses incurred on first lettings
- Post-letting expenses, i.e. expenses incurred after the period of the last letting
- Capital expenditure incurred on additions, alterations or improvements to the premises unless allowable under an incentive scheme.

A deduction can be made only once. If a deduction has already been made in a person's tax computation, the amount will not be allowed as a deduction in arriving at the person's net profit/loss rent (i.e. you cannot obtain relief more than once for the same expense).

Expenses incurred in the letting of premises on an uneconomic basis are not deductible.

Expenses incurred between lettings

Expenses incurred in the period between lettings are deductible provided that the landlord was not in occupation of the premises during the period and a new lease is granted.

Rent-a-Room Relief

Where an individual rents a room (or rooms) in a 'qualifying residence' and the gross rent received, including sums arising for food, laundry or similar goods and services, does not exceed €10,000 (or €7,620 in 2007), this income will be exempt from tax by including it in the individual's tax return. Where more than one individual is entitled to the rent, the limit is divided between the individuals concerned. The relief is available to individuals only. It does not apply to companies or partnerships. However, it can apply where individuals have the income jointly (for instance, a husband and wife where there is no partnership), in which case the limit can be divided between them. Individuals who rent, as well as individuals who own their own home, may avail of the relief.

For 2007 and following years, Rent-a-Room Relief cannot be granted in respect of accommodation provided by parents for their own children. In circumstances where there are non-related persons paying rent for rooms in the family home, these payments will still qualify for Rent-a-Room relief.

A 'qualifying residence' is a residential premises in the State, which is occupied by an individual as his or her principal private residence during the year of assessment. Room rentals coming within the scope of this scheme will not affect the person's entitlement to Mortgage Interest Relief or the Capital Gains Tax exemption on the disposal of a principal private residence.

There is no deduction for expenses made in ascertaining the rental income received. If the income does not exceed the limit in the year, those profits/losses are treated as nil for the year of assessment.

This income is not liable to either PRSI or the Universal Social Charge but it must be included on an individual's annual income tax return. An individual may, if they wish, elect to have any income/losses from this source assessed under the normal rules for rental income, e.g. if there is a rental loss on the room (or rooms). To do this, complete the relevant section on your annual income tax return.

What if a premises is only partly let?

If only part of a premises is let, only expenses incurred on that part of the premises are available for set-off against rental income. For example, if the income received from rooms let in a private house exceeds the limits of the Rent-a-Room Relief, and the expenses for gas, electricity, and so on are shared by all the occupants of the house, only expenses applicable to that part of the house which is let are available for set-off against profit rent. Expenses should be apportioned based on the occupancy of the house (i.e. the number of rooms occupied by tenants).

How is profit/loss rent calculated?

The rental profit or loss is calculated by reference to the rent or total receipts to which the person becomes entitled in any tax year (as opposed to the period to which the income relates).

EXAMPLE

Mr White began leasing a house from Mr Brown on 1 December 2007. Mr White pays rent in installments of €3,000 on the first day of each quarter of the year. He paid €3,000 on 1 December 2007. His landlord, Mr Brown, became entitled to receive the quarter's rent on that date, therefore the entire €3,000 is taxable income for 2007. It is important to note that the €3,000 is not apportioned so as to make two-thirds of it taxable in the tax year 2008.

A separate computation is prepared for each property whereby the rental expenses are deducted from the related income for each property in order to arrive at a surplus (i.e. income greater than expenses) or a deficit (i.e. expenses greater than income). The total of surpluses and deficits is then aggregated to arrive at profits or gains arising in the year, i.e. taxable rent.

What if a loss is made?

A loss will arise if total allowable expenses are more than the rents received. This loss can be set against any other rental profit made by the landlord or carried forward against future rental profits. Such losses cannot be carried back or used to shelter non-rental income.

How is the tax due on rental income collected?

Rental profit is taxed on the basis of the actual tax year. For individuals with rental profits that are relatively small and who are taxed under the PAYE system, the tax can be collected by reducing their tax credits and their standard rate cut-off point. Otherwise, the tax due will be collected under the self-assessment system.

What kind of records should be kept?

You must keep full and accurate records of your lettings from the start. You need to do this whether you send in a simple profit/loss summary, prepare the accounts yourself, or have an accountant do it for you. All supporting records such as invoices, bank or building society statements, cheque stubs and receipts should also be retained. You must keep your records for six years unless your local Revenue office advises you otherwise. See the table on the opposite page for an example of a rent account.

What if rents are payable to a non-resident landlord?

If a landlord resides outside the country and rent is paid directly to him/her or to his/her bank account either in the State or abroad, tax must be deducted by the tenant at the standard rate of tax (currently 20 percent) from the gross rents payable. Note: Failure to deduct tax leaves the tenant liable for the tax which should have been deducted.

Example Rent Account	
INCOME	
Gross rent	€15,000
TOTAL INCOME	€15,000
EXPENSES	
Insurance	€ 800
Ground rent	€ 300
Electricity/heating	€1,200
Repairs	€1,900
Wear and tear (€7,000 x 12.5 percent)	€875
TOTAL EXPENSES	€5,075
PROFIT RENT (TAXABLE RENTAL INCOME)	€9,925

EXAMPLE
Gross rent per month: €1,000
Deduct tax (1,000 x 20 percent): €200
Pay to landlord: €800

At the end of the year, the tenant must also give a completed form R 185 to the landlord to show that the tax has been accounted for to Revenue. The landlord can then claim this amount as credit on their annual tax return.

Where an agent resident in the State is appointed by the non-resident landlord to manage the property and the agent is collecting the rents, the rents must be paid gross to the agent. The agent is then chargeable for tax on the rents and is required to submit an annual tax return and to account for the tax due under self-assessment.

Note: The agent appointed need not be a professional person, i.e. it can be a family member or other person who is prepared to take on the responsibility and to make annual tax returns and account to Revenue for the tax due.

Annual Charge on Non-Principal Private Residences

The Local Government (Charges) Act 2009 has introduced a €200 annual charge for the owners of non-principal private residences. This charge is not administered by the Revenue Commissioners. It is payable by owners to the local authority in whose area the property is located. The charge applies mainly to owners of private rental property and holiday homes. It also applies to vacant residential property, unless newly built but unsold.

Liability to pay the charge is assessed by owners themselves. Ownership of a non-principal private residence on the 'liability date' (31 July, 2009) determines liability to pay the €200 charge.

Mortgage Interest Relief on Rental Income

If at any point you have a mortgage and are in receipt of Tax Relief at Source (TRS), you should advise your local Revenue Office immediately, as you may no longer be entitled to Rent Relief and your Tax Credit Certificate might need to be adjusted.

Capital Gains Tax

Where a property that has been let is disposed of, Capital Gains Tax may arise on the disposal. The chargeable gain is calculated by deducting any allowable expenditure from the amount realised on the disposal. The allowable expenditure may include:

- the cost of acquisition of the property, including fees such as for solicitors or auctioneers
- any costs incurred in improving the value of the property
- any costs of disposal, including fees such as for solicitors or auctioneers

Expenditure on costs of acquisition and improvement may be adjusted to take account of inflation. Where a disposal is made on or after 1 January 2003, the indexation relief will only apply for the period of ownership of the asset up to 31 December 2002. No relief is due if the period of ownership is less than twelve months.

Tax Relief on Loan Interest

Tax Relief at Source (TRS) on secured loans

Tax relief for home mortgage interest (secured loans) is not given through the tax system but is instead granted at source (TRS). Mortgage repayments are reduced by the amount of the tax credit due. For example, if the interest element of your mortgage repayment per month is €500, your mortgage lender will reduce your monthly mortgage payment by €100 per month. This reduction is the same as giving tax relief at the standard rate of tax (20 percent). Any future adjustments in your tax relief will be made automatically by your mortgage lender. It is not necessary to claim relief on your annual tax return or to contact your local Revenue office. If, however, you are making mortgage repayments and *not* receiving Tax Relief at Source, you should contact the TRS Section.

Unsecured Home Loans

Relief for interest payments made on unsecured home loans used for qualifying purposes, i.e. repair or improvement of your sole or main residence, can be claimed by review at the end of the tax year. If, however, you are paying interest on a private residence mortgage in excess of the ceiling for relief (listed below) and are receiving Tax Relief at Source on this interest, there will be no additional relief due in respect of a qualifying unsecured home loan.

Amount of Relief Available

For 2008 for both first-time buyers and non-first-time buyers, Mortgage Interest Relief is due at the standard rate of tax (currently 20 percent), subject to the upper limits in the following chart.

In 2009 and 2010 for first-time buyers, the rate of Mortgage Interest Relief is increased from 20 to 25 percent in years one and two, and to 22.5 percent in years three, four and five. The relief remains unchanged at 20 percent for years six and seven of the mortgage.

For non-first-time buyers, the rate of mortgage relief is reduced from 20 to 15 percent. The higher limits for first-time buyers apply to the tax year in which the mortgage is taken out plus the six following years.

Loans taken out up to 31 December 2011 are eligible for TRS Mortgage Interest Relief until 31 December 2017. Loans taken out from 1 January 2012 to 31 December 2012 will be entitled to Mortgage interest relief at the reduced rates of 15 percent for first time buyers, 10 percent for non first time buyers, per individual on the first €3,000 of interest paid.

Ceilings, 2008, 2009 & 2010		
	First-time buyers	**All others**
Single person	€10,000	€3,000
Married/widowed person	€20,000	€6,000

Tax relief for interest paid on home loans

What is tax relief for interest paid on home loans and who can claim it?

Tax relief is available to an individual who pays interest on a loan which is used purchase, repair, develop or improve a qualifying residence, or to pay off another loan used for that purpose. Note: Expenditure on furniture and removable fittings (e.g. light fittings, curtains, drapes and carpets) does not qualify for tax relief.

The qualifying residence must be situated in the State, Northern Ireland or Great Britain and must be used as the sole or main residence of:

- the claimant
- the claimant's former or separated spouse
- a dependent relative for whom the claimant is being granted Dependent Relative Tax Credit and for whom the residence is provided free of rent or any other consideration.

Sole or main residence

This means the residence which is your home for the greater part of the time. It does not have to be owned by you (i.e. your parents' residence may also be your sole or main residence, if you normally reside there). 'Residence' includes or a house, a flat or a mobile home, provided it:

- is immobilised
- is on a permanent site
- has electricity and other services supplied to it
- is of a reasonable size to fulfil the requirements of use as a permanent residence

First-time buyer

First Time Buyer means an individual who has not previously been entitled to relief in respect of interest paid on loans used for the purchase, repair, development or improvement of an individual's sole or main residence. In the case of joint loans, it is possible for just one of the party to be a first-time buyer.

Relief due

From 2002 onwards, Tax Relief at Source applies to secured home loans used to purchase, repair, develop or improve your sole or main residence. Relief for unsecured loans is granted by review at the end of the tax year and is granted at the standard rate of tax. Separate maximum limits apply depending on whether it is an existing loan or was taken out less than five years ago (seven years with effect from 1 January 2003).

Examples of Qualifying Loans

The loans can have been taken out for:

- extensions, purchase/construction of a garage, garden shed, greenhouse, swimming pool, tennis court
- construction of driveway, path
- conversions, painting and decorating
- installation of central heating
- rewiring, plumbing (including bathroom suites)
- replacing windows and installing double glazing
- purchase and installation of bedroom and kitchen units which are affixed to and become part of the building
- purchase and installation of burglar/fire alarms
- cost of installation and treatment for conditions including damp, dry rot and woodworm

- landscaping gardens (including garden walls)
- contributions to group water and sewerage schemes
- purchase of another person's part-interest in the residence
- legal and other fees incidental to the purchase or development of the residence
- stamp duty on the purchase of a residence.

Mortgage Interest Relief

In 2009, after the mini-budget, the government changed the rules with respect to this relief. Mortgage Interest Relief (Tax Relief at Source, or TRS) is available for the first seven years of a qualifying loan. Note: If you have been in receipt of Mortgage Interest Relief for more than seven years on your current mortgage, you are no longer entitled to TRS with effect from 1 May 2009.

As outlined in Budget 2010, Mortgage Interest Relief has been extended for first-time buyers who are within the first seven years of their mortgage until 2017. First-time buyers will be eligible from now till this time. It also applies to a person buying a new home between now and 1 July 2011 and who qualifies for the relief at current rates. Transitional arrangements will apply to loans taken out in the subsequent eighteen-month period. It is proposed that in 2017 Mortgage Interest Relief will be phased out entirely.

What is a qualifying loan?

A qualifying loan for the purpose of TRS is a secured loan which must be used solely for the purchase, repair, development or improvement of your principal private residence.

EXAMPLE:
Sarah takes out a home loan for €100,000, for which relief is available. Sarah's loan therefore has a qualifying percentage of 100 percent.

Switching lender or mortgage type to achieve a better interest rate does not equate to a new loan. However, if a person moves home and takes out a new mortgage for this home with a new or existing lender, the new mortgage is eligible for relief for seven tax years from the date of first payment.

What is a non-qualifying loan?

A loan used for the purchase of an investment property does not qualify for Mortgage Interest Relief (TRS). If part of your mortgage is used to finance non-home expenditure such as a holiday, car or education, only the percentage relevant to your principal private residence qualifies for Mortgage Interest Relief.

EXAMPLE
Sarah consolidates her personal and home loan borrowings by remortgaging her home. The breakdown is as follows:

Car loan/Personal loan	€ 30,000
Home loan balance	€ 70,000
Total mortgage	€100,000

Relief is available on the home loan balance of €70,000 only, out of total borrowings of €100,000:

€70,000 / €100,000 x 100 = 70 percent

Sarah's loan therefore has a qualifying percentage of 70 percent.

How do I apply for Mortgage Interest Relief (TRS)?

You should wait until you have made your first mortgage repayment before applying for TRS. To claim the relief, you must register your mortgage with Revenue. The most efficient way to complete this registration is online at *www.revenue.ie/en/online/mortgage-interestrelief.html.* Alternatively, follow the link at *www.getyourtaxback.ie.* You can complete a TRS1P form, available from your lender or from Revenue. Upon registration, you should allow up to eight weeks for TRS to be applied on your loan.

How do I claim for previous years?

You may wish to claim relief for prior years (only four previous years can be claimed for). Such claims can also be made on form TRS1P. Claims relating to prior years can only be made after the end of the year in question.

How do I de-register a loan for Mortgage Interest Relief (TRS)?

If your property ceases to be your principal private residence and the mortgage account is not cleared and paid, or if your loan's qualifying percentage changes, you must notify Revenue immediately. You can do this by using a TRS4 form or by contacting the Revenue TRS helpline.

What if your lender is a local authority or credit union?

If your mortgage lender is a local authority (a county, city or town council) or a credit union, you will receive full details directly from your local authority or credit union on how tax relief at source will be applied to your home loan.

How much Mortgage Interest Relief (TRS) is available?

The rates of relief applicable from January 2009 are set out in the table below. Relief is calculated on the qualifying interest on your loan, or on your personal ceiling, whichever is the lesser. The higher limits for first-time buyers apply for the tax year in which the mortgage is taken out plus six subsequent years. Compare your qualifying interest with the relevant ceiling outlined below.

Mortgage Interest Relief rates (in euros)		
	Single	Married/ widowed
Ceiling	10,000	20,000
Rate of relief years 1 and 2	@ 25%	@ 25%
Maximum relief available	2,500	5,000
Rate of relief years 3, 4 and 5	@22.5%	@22.5%
Maximum relief available	2,250	4,500
Rate of relief years 6 and 7	@ 20%	@20%
Maximum relief available	2,000	4,000

How do I apply for Mortgage Interest Relief (TRS)?

After you have made your first mortgage repayment, complete the TRS application and submit your TRS1P to Revenue by post. Correctly completed application forms are input onto the Revenue computer system. Your lender is then notified of the correct ceiling and percentage qualifying for your loan. Your lender calculates relief due to you based on your interest payments and information supplied by Revenue. It can take up to eight weeks for Mortgage Interest Relief (TRS) to be applied to your account.

6

Relief for Medical Expenses

What is this relief and to whom does it apply?

Tax relief may be claimed for certain medical expenses paid by you. From 2007 onwards, you may claim tax relief in respect of any qualifying health expenses paid by you in respect of any individuals. Prior to 2007, tax relief could only be claimed in respect of health expenses paid by you on behalf of yourself, a dependant, or a relative. Most medical expenses (with some exceptions, e.g. routine dental and ophthalmic care) qualify for relief. All qualifying and non-qualifying reliefs are explained below. You cannot claim for any expenditure which has been, or will be, reimbursed by an authorised medical insurer, e.g. Hibernian, Quinn or VHI, or where a compensation payment is made or will be made.

A dependant is any relative of yours or any other person in your care who at any time during the year of claim is aged sixty-five years or over or who is permanently incapacitated by reason of mental or physical infirmity.

A relative is defined as: a husband, wife, ancestor, lineal descendant, brother or sister; the mother or father of your spouse; the brother or sister of your spouse; the spouse of your son or daughter; your child, or any other child who in the year of the claim is in your custody, is maintained at your expense and is under eighteen years of age, or, if over eighteen, is in full-time education.

What expenditure qualifies for relief?

- Doctors and consultants fees
- Items or treatments prescribed by a doctor or consultant (see below)
- Maintenance or treatment in a hospital or an approved nursing home
- Costs of speech and language therapy carried out by a speech and language therapist for a qualifying child
- Costs of educational psychological assessments carried out by an educational psychologist for a qualifying child (allowable from 6 April 2001)
- Transport by ambulance.

Relief for Educational Psychologists and Speech and Language Therapy

Relief is available for expenditure incurred in respect of qualifying dependants (children) for the services of an educational psychologist or a speech and language therapist.

An educational psychologist is a person who is entered on a register maintained by the Minister for Education and Science in accordance with guidelines set down by that Minister. A copy of the current register is available from your local Revenue office.

A speech and language therapist is a person approved by the Minister for Health and Children in accordance with guidelines set down by that Minister. Speech and language therapists are not included on a register but confirmation of approval can be obtained from the Department of Health and Children.

Relief for Travelling and Accommodation Expenses

Relief in respect of transport expenses within the State is restricted to expenses of transport by ambulance, except in certain circumstances. Where regular continuing treatment or consultation is required and the patient has to travel long distances, the expenses may be admitted. It is not the intention that minor local travelling expenses or occasional travelling (unless by ambulance), e.g. to undergo an operation, be admitted.

Where qualifying health care is obtainable only outside the State, reasonable expenses of travelling and accommodation for the patient may be allowed. In such a case, the expenses of one person accompanying the patient may also be allowed where the condition of the patient requires it. If the patient is a child, the expenses of one parent may generally be allowed and, exceptionally, the expenses of both parents where both have to be in attendance.

Health Expenses which may be claimed by Kidney Patients

In the case of kidney patients, tax relief may be claimed on *the expenses outlined below. Note: It is possible for a patient to move from one category to another. Where this happens, relief for each category may be apportioned as appropriate.*

Hospital dialysis patients (where the patient attends hospital for treatment)

Relief in respect of expenditure incurred travelling to and from hospital (unlimited journeys for all years) may be allowed at the following rates:

2006 - €0.35 per mile
2007 - €0.36 per mile or €0.23 per kilometre
2008 - €0.36 per mile or €0.23 per kilometre
2009 - €0.27 per mile or €0.17 per kilometre

Home dialysis patients (where the patient uses a dialysis machine at home)

Relief may be allowed in respect of expenditure up to the following amounts:

	2009	2008	2007	2006
Electricity	€1,665	€1,935	€1,565	€1,505
Laundry and protective clothing	€1,940	€2,030	€1,950	€1,855
Telephone	€301	€315	€300	€285
Travel	€0.27 per mile €0.17 per km	€0.36 per mile €0.23 per km	€0.36 per mile €0.23 per km	€0.35 per mile €0.22 per km

Chronic ambulatory peritoneal dialysis (CAPD) patients (where the patient has treatment at home without the use of a dialysis machine)

Relief may be allowed in respect of expenditure incurred up to the following amounts:

	2009	2008	2007	2006
Electricity	€1,315	€1,530	€1,235	€1,185
Telephone	€301	€315	€300	€285
Travel	€0.27 per mile €0.17 per km	€0.36 per mile €0.23 per km	€0.36 per mile €0.23 per km	€0.35 per mile €0.22 per km

Relief for Child Health-care Expenses

Certain items of expenditure in respect of children suffering from a serious, life-threatening illness (including child oncology patients) and children with permanent disabilities who require constant or regular hospital care qualify for relief.

Travel

Relief is available to offset the cost incurred in transporting the child and accompanying parents/guardians to and from any approved hospital, and the cost incurred by the parents/guardians of the child in visiting the hospital when the child is an inpatient where such trips are shown to be essential to the treatment of the child. If a private car is used, the cost of travel is determined at the rates outlined previously for kidney patients.

Telephone

Where the child is being treated at home, a flat rate of €300, to include telephone rental and calls, may be claimed where the expenses are incurred for purposes directly connected with the treatment of the child. The rates available in previous years are as follows:

2010	2009	2008	2007	2006
€300	€301	€315	€300	€285

Overnight accommodation

Relief is available for payments made by the parent/guardian to a hospital, hotel or B&B in respect of overnight accommodation in or near the hospital where the child is a patient, where such overnight stay is necessary for the treatment of the child.

Note: Claims in respect of the cost of minding brothers/sisters of the patient while the parents/guardians attend the hospital are not allowable.

Hygiene products and special clothing

The cost incurred in respect of these items, subject to a maximum of €500 per year.

In-vitro Fertilisation

For the purposes of Section 469 TCA 1997, in-vitro fertilisation may be regarded as 'treatment in respect of infertility', and relief may be allowed against the cost of this treatment, where it is carried out by a practitioner (within the meaning of Section 469).

If the treatment involves maintenance in a hospital (i.e. overnight), relief may be allowed in respect of any expenditure incurred where the hospital is on the Revenue list of approved hospitals.

General Medical Expenses

The following, *where prescribed by a doctor*, qualify for medical expenses relief:

- drugs and medicines

- diagnostic procedures
- orthoptic or similar treatment
- hearing aids
- orthopaedic bed/chair
- wheelchair/wheelchair lift (no relief is due for alterations to the building to facilitate a lift)
- glucometer machine for a diabetic
- engaging a qualified nurse in the case of a serious illness
- physiotherapy or similar treatment
- cost of a computer where it is necessary to alleviate communication problems experienced by a severely handicapped person
- cost of gluten-free food for coeliacs. As this condition is generally ongoing, a letter (rather than prescriptions) from a doctor stating that the individual is a coeliac sufferer is acceptable. Receipts from supermarkets in addition to receipts from chemists are acceptable.

What relief is available?

Up to 2007, there was no compensation given for the first €125 for a single person or €250 for a spouse and dependants. From 2007 onwards, there is no lower limit.

How do I claim?

Tax relief can be claimed after 31 December of the year of claim. A claim may be made by completing and submitting a Med 1 form at the end of the tax year to your local Revenue office. You should also send in evidence of payment of tax for that year (P60 form in the case of a PAYE employee – both P60 forms in the case of both spouses working and jointly assessed for tax). *There is no need to submit receipts with your claim, but only expenditure for which you hold receipts can be claimed.*

If you are claiming dental expenses, a completed Med 2 form should be obtained from your dental practitioner. These receipts and Med 2 form must be retained for a period of six years, as you may be asked to produce the forms if your claim is chosen for detailed examination.

When is relief given?

You can choose whether you want the relief given for the year in which the payments were made or for the year in which the expenses were incurred.

EXAMPLE
A hospital stay in December 2004 cost €635. €380 was paid in December 2004 and €255 was paid in May 2005. You can claim relief in either of the following ways:

€635 (less €125) in the tax year 2004 or;
€380 (less €125) in the tax year 2004 and €255 (less €125) in the tax year 2005

Up to 31 December 2008, relief is granted at the highest rate of tax at which you are liable for the year of claim. From 2009 onwards, relief is only available at the standard rate of tax.

If your subscription year for medical insurance (VHI, Quinn Healthcare, VIVAS Health, etc) does not coincide with the tax year, you may submit your claim based on the subscription year. Expenses in the subscription year will be treated as having been incurred in the calendar year in which the subscription year ends. However, claims for subsequent tax years must also be based on your subscription year.

Drugs and Medicine Relief

From 1 January 2010, you can claim tax relief for expenditure of amounts up to €120 per calendar month for prescribed medication. Expenditure in excess of €120 per month is recoverable from the HSE under the drugs payment scheme. The amounts recoverable for periods prior to 1 January 2010 are as follows:

1 January 2004 to 31 December 2004:	€ 78
1 January 2005 to 31 December 2007:	€ 85
1 January 2008 to 31 December 2008:	€ 90
1 January 2009 to 31 December 2009:	€100
1 January 2010 to 31 December 2010:	€120

You can get a Med 1 form from your local doctor.

Dental Treatments which Qualify for Relief

BRIDGEWORK

Dental treatment consisting of an enamel-retained bridge or a tooth-supported bridge is allowable.

CROWNS

These are restorations fabricated outside the mouth and are permanently cemented to existing tooth tissue.

TIP REPLACING

This is regarded as a crown, where a large part of the tooth needs to be replaced and the replacement is made outside the mouth.

VENEERS/REMBRANT-TYPE ETCHED FILLINGS

These are a form of crown.

ENDODONTICS (ROOT CANAL TREATMENT)

This involves the filling of the nerve canal and not the filling of teeth.

GOLD INLAYS

These are a smaller version of a gold crown and are only allowable if fabricated outside the mouth.

GOLD POSTS

These are inserts in the nerve canal of a tooth, to hold a crown.

ORTHODONTIC TREATMENT

This involves the provision of braces and/or similar treatments.

PERIODONTAL TREATMENT

- Root planing - a treatment of periodontal (gum) disease
- Currettage and debridement - part of root planing
- Gum flaps - a gum treatment
- Chrome cobalt splint - if used in connection with periodontal treatment. (If it contains teeth, relief is not allowable.)
- Dental implants following treatment of periodontal (gum) disease, which included bone grafting and bone augmentation.

EXTRACTION OF IMPACTED WISDOM TEETH

Relief is allowable when undertaken in a hospital, or by a dentist in a dental surgery. Certification from the hospital/dentist will be required to obtain tax relief. *The removal of teeth in any other circumstances does not qualify.*

What treatments do not qualify for relief?

Tax relief is *not* available for scaling, extraction and filling of teeth or the provision and repair of artificial teeth and dentures.

Routine Ophthalmic Care

Tax relief is not available for the cost of sight testing, provision and maintenance of spectacles and contact lenses.

How to claim

Claims in respect of dental treatments can be made by completing a Med 2 form and forwarding it to your local Revenue office.

Medical Insurance Premiums

What is relief on medical insurance premiums and to whom does it apply?

If you pay medical insurance to an authorised insurer (see list below), you are entitled to tax relief. Ordinarily, this relief is granted at source by your medical insurer. Subscribers to medical insurance will pay a reduced premium – 80 percent of the gross amount – to the insurer. The reduction is the same as giving tax relief at the standard rate of 20 percent. Please check with your insurer that you are receiving this relief.

In cases where medical premiums are paid by an employer on behalf of their employee as a benefit in kind, tax relief will not have been allowed at source. Tax relief can be claimed from the Revenue.

Authorised Insurers

- Aviva Health Insurance Ireland Ltd.
- ESB Staff Medical Provident Fund

- Goulding Voluntary Medical Scheme
- HSF Health Plan Ltd.
- Irish Life Assurance (plc) Medical Aid Society
- Irish Life Assurance (plc) Outdoor Staff Benevolent Fund
- Prison Officers Medical Aid Society
- Quinn Healthcare
- St Pauls Garda Medical Aid Society
- VHI

How do I claim the relief?

Contact your local Revenue office and complete an annual return form.

Relief for Revenue-approved Permanent Health Benefit Schemes

What is this relief and to whom does it apply?

An individual who pays a premium on a policy to secure the continuance of income and payment of benefits during disablement through accident, injury or sickness can claim this relief. The policy must be approved by the Revenue Commissioners as a Permanent Health Benefit Scheme.

What relief is available?

Relief is given at the higher rate of tax which a person pays.

How can I claim the relief?

Where an employer deducts the contributions from gross pay, the tax relief is given at source, so no further action is necessary to claim relief. Where an employer does not deduct the contributions from gross pay, relief can be claimed from the Revenue by means of an adjustment on a person's tax relief certificate.

The relief is allowed in respect of premiums paid in the year. Only the portion of the contribution or premium that relates to the provision of Permanent Health Benefit applies.

A net pay basis applies to premiums paid by PAYE workers, i.e. the contribution will be deducted from the gross pay before tax is calculated.

7

Calculating All Your Reliefs and Making Your Claim

Over the last few chapters, I have shown you the various reliefs that are available and how to calculate your tax liability. Now you must put all that information together so that you can submit your claim. As you have seen, some reliefs can be claimed instantly; others as part of an end-of-year review. For those end-of-year reviews, please be aware that in cases which are retrospective there are deadlines. This of course will only matter for the last year of your claim.

I would suggest simply that you get a small safe or secure box in which, throughout the year, you put all your payslips, tax credit certificate, P60, medical receipts and any other relevant documents. Then at the beginning of the following year, take the time to go through it all and make your claim. For most reliefs you do not have to submit the receipts, but these must be retained for a period of six years. Also take the time to do a review of not just your PAYE but also of your PRSI contributions. This is an area that is sometimes overlooked, but on review can be rewarding.

If there are some areas that you do not fully understand, this should not worry you. Once you are aware of your possible entitlement and its existence, then when the time comes to do your end-of-year review, you will be able to query whether or not you are entitled to claim it.

Now that you know what you are entitled to, there are a number of different ways to submit your claim. There are online companies who will do it for you on your behalf – for a fee, of course. Alternatively, I would suggest using the Revenue-online system, which is free to use. This will suit those of you who have internet access. For those of you who do not have access to the internet or do not trust your internet skills, I would suggest contacting your local Revenue office and supplying them with all the relevant information. Below, I have included a table of relief which will allow you to calculate approximately how much relief is due to you; this will also help you when contacting your Revenue office. Please note that this is a guide only.

	2011	2010	2009	2008	2007
Personal Tax Credits					
Single person's credit	1,830	1,830	1,830	1,830	1,760
My credit					
Married person's credit	3,300	3,660	3,660	3,660	3,520
My credit					
PAYE Credits					
	1,830	1,830	1,830	1,830	1,760
My credit					
Widowed Person's Reliefs					
(Other years) with dependent children	2,190	1,830	1,830	1,830	1,760
My credit					
Without dependent children	2,190	2,430	2,430	2,430	2,310
My credit					
Bereavement year (no dependent children)	2,190	3,660	3,660	3,660	3,520
My credit					

	2011	2010	2009	2008	2007
Widowed Parent – 1st year after death	3,600	4,000	4,000	4,000	3,750
My credit					
Widowed Parent – 2nd year after death	3,150	3,500	3,500	3,500	3,250
My credit					
Widowed Parent – 3rd year after death	2,700	3,000	3,000	3,000	2,750
My credit					
Widowed Parent – 4th year after death	2,250	2,500	2,500	2,500	2,250
My credit					
Widowed Parent – 5th year after death	1,800	1,830	1,830	1,830	1,760
My credit					
Single Parent Credits					
Single Parent Family Credit	1,650	1,830	1,830	1,830	1,760
My credit					

	2011	2010	2009	2008	2007
Single Parent Widowed Credit	1,650	1,830	1,830	1,830	1,760
My credit					
Age Tax Credits					
Age Tax Credit, single	245	325	325	325	275
My credit					
Age Tax Credit, married	490	650	650	650	550
My credit					
Home Carer's Credits					
Home Carer's Credit (Max)	810	900	900	900	770
Incapacitated and Dependent Person's Credits					
Incapacitated person employing a carer (max)	50,000	50,000	50,000	50,000	50,000
My credit					
Incapacitated child	3,300	3,660	3,660	3,660	3,000
My credit					

	2011	2010	2009	2008	2007
Dependent relative	70	80	80	80	80
My credit					
Dependent relative income limit	13,837	13,837	13,837	13,473	12,745
My credit					
Blind Person's Credits and Allowances					
Blind person, one spouse blind	1,650	1,830	1,830	1,830	1,760
My credit					
Blind person, both spouses blind	3,300	3,660	3,660	3,660	3,520
My credit					
Guide dog allowance	825	825	825	825	825
My credit					
Revenue Job Assist Credits					
Year 1 (additional for each child)	3,810 (1,270)	3,810 (1,270)	3,810 (1,270)	3,810 (1,270)	3,810 (1,270)
My credit					

	2011	2010	2009	2008	2007
Year 2 (additional for each child)	2,540 (850)	2,540 (850)	2,540 (850)	2,540 (850)	2,540 (850)
My credit					
Year 3 (additional for each child)	1,270 (425)	1,270 (425)	1,270 (425)	1,270 (425)	1,270 (425)
My credit					
Rent Tax Credit					
Single, under fifty-five	320	400	400	400	360
Single, over fifty-five	640	800	800	800	720
My credit					
Married, under fifty-five	640	800	800	800	720
Married, over fifty-five	1,280	1,600	1,600	1,600	1,440
My credit					
Widowed, under fifty-five	640	800	800	800	720
Widowed, over fifty-five	1,280	1,600	1,600	1,600	1,440
My credit					

	2011	2010	2009	2008	2007
Trade Union Subscription Tax Credit					
Trade Union Subscription Credit	Abolished	70	70	70	60
My credit					
Tax Credit Rates for Service Charges					
Tags/independent contractor	Abolished	80	80	80	80
My credit					

Appendix A

List of Relevant Forms for Claiming Tax Reliefs and Allowances

Incapacitated Child Relief	Form IT 18
Blind Person's Relief and VAT exemptions	Form IT 35
Revenue Job Assist	Form IT 58
Claim for Dependant Relative Tax Credit	Form IT 46
Claim for Dependant Relative Tax Credit - employing a carer	Form IT 47
Claim for Home Carer's Relief	Form IT 66
Age Tax Credit	Form IT 45
One Parent Family Tax Credit	Form OP 1
Personal Tax Return	Form 12
Claim for Rent Relief for Private Rented Accommodation	Rent 1
Relief for Tuition Fees	Form IT31
Relief for Service Charges	Form IT 27
Claim for Repayment of Tax during Unemployment	Form P 50
Claim for Medical Expenses	Form Med 1
Claim for Dental Expenses	Form Med 2
Claim for Relief for Medical Insurance	Form IT 5

Appendix B

Local Revenue Office Contact Details

Throughout the book, I state that in order to see if you qualify for certain reliefs you must contact your local Revenue office and supply the relevant details. The country is divided into four regions, each of which deals with their respective area. The regions are as follows:

- Dublin Region: covers both Dublin City and County
- East & Southeast Region: covers Carlow, Kildare, Kilkenny, Laois, Meath, Tipperary, Waterford, Wexford and Wicklow
- Southwest Region: covers Clare, Cork, Kerry and Limerick
- Border, Midlands, West Region: covers Cavan, Donegal, Galway, Leitrim, Longford, Louth, Mayo, Monaghan, Offaly, Roscommon, Sligo and Westmeath

All the above section are divided up into districts. Below is listed all contact details for each local office in each region. I have included the address, phone number and email address for each.

Dublin Region

The Dublin City and County is broken up as follows:

DUBLIN CITY CENTRE OFFICE
9/15 Upper O'Connell Street, Dublin 1

LoCall No. for PAYE Customers: 1890 333 425
Customer service for PAYE customers: citycentrepaye @revenue.ie

SOUTH CITY OFFICE

This office covers the Dublin City Council local authority area south of River Liffey, excluding Dublin 2 postal district.

85-93 Lower Mount St, Dublin 2
LoCall No. for PAYE Customers: 1890 333 425
Customer service for PAYE customers: Dublinsouthcitypaye @revenue.ie

NORTH CITY OFFICE

This office covers the Dublin City Council local authority area north of River Liffey, excluding Dublin 1 postal district.

9/15 Upper O'Connell St, Dublin 1
LoCall No. for PAYE Customers: 1890 333 425
Customer service for PAYE customers: dublinnorthcitypaye@ revenue.ie

SOUTH COUNTY OFFICE

This office covers all taxes and duties of customers living in and businesses managed and controlled in South Dublin County Council local authority area.

Plaza Complex, Belgard Rd, Tallaght, Dublin 24
LoCall No. for PAYE Customers: 1890 333 425
Customer service for PAYE customers: southcountypaye@ revenue.ie

FINGAL OFFICE

This office covers all taxes and duties of customers living in and businesses managed and controlled in Fingal County Council local authority area.

Block D Ashtown Gate, Navan Rd, Dublin 15
LoCall No. for PAYE Customers: 1890 333 425

Customer service for PAYE customers: fingalpaye@revenue.ie

DUN LAOGHAIRE-RATHDOWN OFFICE
This office covers all taxes and duties of customers living in and businesses managed and controlled in the Dun Laoghaire-Rathdown Council local authority area.

Lansdowne House, Lansdowne Rd, Dublin 4
LoCall No. for PAYE Customers: 1890 333 425
Customer service for PAYE customers: dlrp@revenue.ie

East and South East Region

The East and South East Region comprises Counties Carlow, Kilkenny, Kildare, Laois, Meath, Tipperary, Waterford, Wexford and Wicklow. Persons living in these counties and businesses managed and controlled within these counties will have their tax and duty affairs dealt with in the East and South East Region.

The region is sub-divided for administrative purposes into Revenue districts, loosely based around county lines. For the most part therefore, your point of contact will be the District in which you reside.

In the East and South East Region, there is a single correspondence address for all PAYE contacts, a single LoCall phone number for telephone enquiries, a single fax number and a single email address for PAYE customers. There is also a local office at each location, the details of which are listed below also.

EAST AND SOUTH EAST OFFICE
PAYE Mail Centre, P.O. Box 1, Rosslare Harbour, County Wexford
LoCall No. for PAYE Customers: 1890 444 425
Customer service for PAYE customers: esePAYE@revenue.ie

For PAYE customers who wish to do business through Irish:
046 9033517
esePAYEgaeilge@revenue.ie

EAST AND SOUTH EAST REGIONAL OFFICE

The East and South East Regional Office is responsible for the management and administration of the East and South East Region.

Government Offices, The Glen, Waterford
051 862100
Customer service for PAYE customers:
eseregionaloffice@revenue.ie

EAST AND SOUTH EAST REGION - REVENUE DISTRICTS

WATERFORD DISTRICT

This Revenue District covers the entire county of Waterford, the Clonmel area of South Tipperary and South Kilkenny. It deals with customer services including PAYE

Government Offices, The Glen, Waterford
051 862100
customer service for PAYE customers: waterford@revenue.ie

Civic Offices, Dungarvan, County Waterford
058 48154
dungarvan@revenue.ie

The Quay, Clonmel, County Tipperary
052 70270
clonmel@revenue.ie

WEXFORD DISTRICT

The Wexford Revenue District covers County Wexford. It deals with customer services, including PAYE.
Government Offices, Anne Street, Wexford (Monday to Friday: 10:00–16:00)
053 9149300
wexford@revenue.ie

KILKENNY DISTRICT

The Kilkenny Revenue District covers Counties Carlow, Laois and Kilkenny, but excludes South Kilkenny which is covered by Waterford District. It deals with customer services, including PAYE.

Government Offices, Hebron Road, Kilkenny (Monday to Friday: 10:00–16:00)
056 7783700
kilkenny@revenue.ie

6/8 Staplestown Road, Carlow
056 7783700
kilkenny@revenue.ie

KILDARE DISTRICT

The Kildare Revenue District covers County Kildare. It deals with customer services, including PAYE.

Athy Business Campus, Castlecomer Road, Athy, County Kildare
059 8643200
kildarecustomerservice@revenue.ie

TIPPERARY DISTRICT

The Tipperary Revenue District covers County Tipperary, except for the area around and including Clonmel that is covered by the Waterford District. It deals with customer services (including PAYE).

Government Offices, Stradavoher, Thurles, County Tipperary (Monday to Friday: 9:30–17:00)
0504 59500
thurles@revenue.ie
ACC Building, Liberty Square, Thurles, County Tipperary
0504 22009

MEATH DISTRICT

The Meath Revenue District covers the entire county of Meath. It deals with customer services, including PAYE.

Abbey Buildings, Abbey Road, Navan, County Meath (Monday–Friday: 10.00–16.00)
046 9033600
meath@revenue.ie

WICKLOW DISTRICT
The Wicklow Revenue District covers County Wicklow. It deals with customer services, including PAYE.

4 Claremont Road, Sandymount, Dublin 4
01 6316500
wicklow@revenue.ie

Government Offices, The Murrough, Wicklow
0404 60200

South West Region

The region is sub-divided into Revenue districts responsible for customer service, compliance and audit functions for the taxes and duties for persons living in and businesses managed and controlled in its geographical area.

In the South West Region, there is a single correspondence address for all PAYE contacts and a single LoCall Telephone number for telephone enquiries for PAYE customers.

ADDRESS AND TELEPHONE NUMBER FOR ALL PAYE CONTACTS
Office of the Revenue Commissioners, South West Region, PAYE Mail Centre, P.O. Box No. 63, Ennis, County Clare
LoCall 1890 222 425
SWPAYE@revenue.ie
REGIONAL OFFICE
Revenue House, Assumption Road, Blackpool, Cork
021 602 7000
swregoffice@revenue.ie

Cork District

This district deals with all taxes and duties of customers living in and businesses managed and controlled in Cork East, Cork South West, Cork North West including PAYE.

Cork East

(Including Cork County East, City North and City Centre customer service)

Revenue House, Assumption Road, Blackpool, Cork (Monday–Friday: 8:30–16:00)
021 602 7000
corkeast@revenue.ie

Cork South West

(Including Cork County South West and City South and City East Customer Service)

Revenue House, Assumption Road, Blackpool, Cork (Monday–Friday: 8:30–16:00)
021 602 7000
corksouthwest@revenue.ie

Cork North West

(Including Cork County North West and City West Customer Service)

Revenue House, Assumption Road, Blackpool, Cork (Monday–Friday: 8:30–16:00)
021 602 7000
corknorthwest@revenue.ie

Limerick

This office deals with all taxes and duties of customers living in and businesses managed and controlled in Limerick.

River House, Charlotte's Quay, Limerick (Monday–Friday: 8:30–16:00)
061 212 700
limerickdistrict@revenue.ie

CLARE
This office deals with all taxes and duties of customers living in and businesses managed and controlled in Clare.

Government Offices, Kilrush Road, Ennis, County Clare
065 6849000
claredistrict@revenue.ie

KERRY
This office deals with all taxes and duties of customers living in and businesses managed and controlled in Kerry.

Government Offices, Spa Road, Tralee, County Kerry (Monday–Friday: 9:15–17:00)
066 7161000
kerrydistrict@revenue.ie

Border, Midlands, West Region

This region is sub-divided into Revenue districts responsible for customer service, compliance and audit functions for the taxes and duties for persons living in and businesses managed and controlled in its geographical area.

Border, Midlands, West Regional also has a single contact number for PAYE enquiries. The number to call is a LoCall Number: 1890 777 425.

BORDER, MIDLANDS, WEST REGIONAL OFFICE
Geata na Cathrach, Fair Green, Galway
091 576350
bmwregion@revenue.ie

GALWAY COUNTY
Geata na Cathrach, Fairgreen, Galway (Monday–Friday: 8:30–16:00)
091 547700
galwaycounty@revenue.ie

Galway City
Geata na Cathrach, Fairgreen, Galway (Monday–Friday: 8:30–16:00)
091 547700
galwayroscommon@revenue.ie

Roscommon
Customer Service/PAYE – Roscommon (all correspondence through Galway office)

Geata na Cathrach, Fairgreen, Galway (Monday–Friday: 8:30–16:00)
091 547700
galwayroscommonPAYE@revenue.ie

Mayo
Michael Davitt House, Castlebar, County Mayo (Monday–Friday: 10:00–16:00)
094 903 7000
mayo@revenue.ie

Sligo
(includes Counties Sligo, Leitrim and Longford)

Government Offices, Cranmore Road, Sligo (Monday–Friday: 10:00–16:00)
071-914 8600
sligo@revenue.ie

Donegal
Government Offices, High Road, Letterkenny, County Donegal (Monday–Friday: 10:00–16:00)
074 916 9400
donegal@revenue.ie
Westmeath/Offaly
Government Offices, Pearse Street, Athlone, County Westmeath
090-6421 800
westmeathoffaly@revenue.ie

LOUTH
Government Offices, Millennium Centre, Dundalk, County Louth
(Monday–Friday: 10:00–16:00)
042-9353700
louth@revenue.ie

CAVAN/MONAGHAN
Government Offices, Millennium Centre, Dundalk, County Louth
042 9353700
cavanmonaghan@revenue.ie

Appendix C

Flat Rate Expenses

	2010	2009	2008 €	2007 €	2006 €	2005 €
Agricultural Advisers (employed by Teagasc)	671	671	671	600	600	600
Archaeologists: (Civil Service)	127	127	127	127	127	127
Architects employed by						
(a) Civil Service	127	127	127	127	127	127
(b) Local Authorities	127	127	127	127	127	127
Airline Cabin Crews	64	64	64	64	64	64
Bar trade: Employees	93	93	93	93	93	93
Building Industry						
Bricklayer	175	175	175	175	175	175
Fitter mechanic, plasterer	103	103	103	103	103	103
Electrician	153	153	153	153	153	153
Mason, roofer slater, tiler, floor layer, stone cutter	120	120	120	120	120	120
Driver, scaffolder, sheeter, steel erector	52	52	52	52	52	52
Professionals: engineers, surveyors, etc.	33	33	33	33	33	33
General operatives (labourers etc. incl. Public Sector)	97	97	97	97	97	97
Bus, rail and road operatives in						
Bus Atha Cliath, Bus Eireann and Iarnod Eireann	160	160	160	160	160	160
Cardiac Technicians						
Female	212	212	212	212	212	212
Male	107	107	107	107	107	107
Carpentry and joinery trades						
Cabinet makers, Carpenters, Joiners	220	220	220	220	220	220
Painters, Polishers, Upholsterers, Wood Cutting Machinists	140	140	140	140	140	140
Civil Service						
Architectural Technologists & Assistants	166	166	166	166	166	166
Clerks of Works (incl. Senior and District Inspectors)	142	142	142	142	142	142
Engineering Technicians for Archaeologists, Architects, Engineers and Surveyors	166	166	166	166	166	166
Park Rangers and constables employed by the Office of Public Works	77	77	77	77	65	65
Clergymen (Church of Ireland)	127	127	127	127	127	127
Consultants (hospital)	695	695	695	695	695	534
Note: Deduction includes subscription to the Irish Medical Council						
Cosmetologists						
Obliged to supply and launder their own white uniforms	160	160	160	160	160	160
Dentists in employment	376	376	376	376	376	376
Dockers	73	73	73	73	73	73
Doctors (hospital, including consultants)	695	695	695	695	695	534
Note: Deduction includes subscription to the Irish Medical Council.						
Draughtsmen (Local Authority)	133	133	133	133	133	133
Driving Instructors	125	125				
Note: This amount represents an annual allocation of half the biannual statutory ADI fee payable to the Road Safety Authority						
Engineers employed by:						

(a) Civil Service	166	166	166	166	166	166
(b) Local Authorities	127	127	127	127	127	127
(c) Eircom, Coillte, OPW	166	166	166	166	166	166
Engineering Industry [and Electrical Industry from 1997/98]						
Skilled workers who bear the full cost of own tools and overalls	331	331	318	318	318	280
Semi-skilled workers who bear the full cost of own tools and overalls	254	254	244	244	244	215
All unskilled workers and skilled or semi-skilled workers who do not bear the full cost of own tools and overalls	219	219	210	210	210	185
Firefighters Full-time	272	272	272	272	272	250
Firefighters Part-time	407	407	407	407	407	375
Fishermen in Employment	318	318	318	318	318	318
Foresters employed by Coillte	166	166	166	166	166	166
Freelance actors chargeable to PAYE	750	750	750	750	750	750
Grooms (Racehorse Training)	294	294	294	294	294	294
Home Helps (Employed directly or indirectly by Health Boards)	256	256	256	256	256	236
Hospitals Domestic Staff:						
To include general operatives, porters, drivers, drivers, attendants, domestics, laundry operatives, cooks, catering supervisors, waitresses, catering staff, kitchen porters						
(a) who are responsible for providing and laundering their own uniforms.	353	353	353	353	353	325
(b) who are obliged to launder the uniforms supplied	185	185	185	185	185	170
(c) whose uniforms are supplied and laundered free	93	93	93	93	93	85
Hotel industry						
Head hall porter	90	90	90	90	90	90
Hall porter	64	64	64	64	64	64
Head waiter	127	127	127	127	127	127
Waiter	97	97	97	97	97	97
Waitress	64	64	64	64	64	64
Chef	97	97	97	97	97	97
Manager	191	191	191	191	191	191
Assistant Manager	127	127	127	127	127	127
Trainee Manager	78	78	78	78	78	78
Kitchen Porter	21	21	21	21	21	21
Journalists						
Journalists, including those in public relations area of journalism	381	381	381	381	381	381
Journalists who receive expense allowances from their employers	153	153	153	153	153	153
Local Authorities						
Executive Chemists	115	115	115	115	115	115
Parks Superintendents	40	40	40	40	40	40
Town Planners	115	115	115	115	115	115
Mining Industry						
(a)miners/shift bosses underground, mill process workers/shift bosses and steam cleaners	1312	1312	1155	1155	1155	1018
(surface workers)	655	655	576	576	576	508

Motor repair and motor assembly trades						
Assembly workers, greasers, storemen and general workers						
(a) who bear the full cost of own tools and overalls	52	52	52	52	52	52
(b) who do not bear the full cost of own tools and overalls	42	42	42	42	42	42
Fitters and mechanics						
(a) who bear the full cost of own tools and overalls	85	85	85	85	85	85
(b) who do not bear the full cost of own tools and overalls	42	42	42	42	42	42
Panel Beaters (See Panel Beaters/Sheet Metal Workers						
Nurses:						
(a) where obliged to supply and launder their own uniforms	733	733	733	733	733	572
(b) where obliged to supply their own uniforms but laundered free	638	638	638	638	638	496
(c) where obliged to launder the uniforms supplied	353	353	353	353	353	280
(d) where uniforms are supplied and laundered by hospital	258	258	258	258	258	205
Nurses: Short Term Contracts through an Agency. Additional Amount Due	80	80	80	80	80	64
Nursing Assistants(including attendants, orderlies and nurses' aides)						
(a) where obliged to supply and launder their own uniforms	526	526	526	526	526	485
(b) where obliged to supply their own uniforms but laundered free	440	440	440	440	440	405
(c) where obliged to launder the uniforms supplied	234	234	234	234	234	215
(d) where uniforms are supplied and laundered by hospital	93	93	93	93	93	85
Occupational Therapists						
(a) where obliged to supply and launder their own uniforms	217	217	217	217	217	217
(b) where obliged to supply their own uniforms but laundered free	153	153	153	153	153	153
(c) where uniforms are supplied and laundered by hospital	52	52	52	52	52	52
Panel Beaters / Sheet metal Workers						
(a) Who bear full cost of own tools and overalls	78	78	78	78	78	78
(b) Who do not bear full cost of own tools and overalls	40	40	40	40	40	40
Pharmacists	450	450	160	160	160	160
Pharmaceutical Assistants (formerly known as Assistant Pharmacists)	250	250	97	97	97	97
NOTE These amounts represent the Annual Retention Fee payable to the PSI						
Physiotherapists						
(a) where obliged to supply and launder their own uniforms	381	381	381	381	381	381

(b) where obliged to supply their own uniforms but laundered free	318	318	318	318	318	318
(c) where uniforms are supplied and laundered by hospital	64	64	64	64	64	64
Pilots (Aer Lingus Group Pilots)	275	275	275	275	275	191
Plumbing trades						
Plumber (non-welder)	177	177	177	177	177	177
Plumber-welder	205	205	205	205	205	205
Pipe fitter-welder	205	205	205	205	205	205
Printing Bookbinding and allied trades						
Bookbinders (Hand)	109	109	109	109	109	109
Bookbinders (Others)	97	97	97	97	97	97
Compositors, linotype and monotype operators	121	121	121	121	121	121
Copy Holders, photo lithographers, photo engravers and workers in T and E section of newspapers	114	114	114	114	114	114
Monotype caster attendants, stereotypes and machine minders	135	135	135	135	135	135
Readers and revisers	100	100	100	100	100	100
Rotary machine minders and assistants	150	150	150	150	150	150
Others (e.g. cutters, dispatchers, rulers, warehousemen)	90	90	90	90	90	90
Professional Valuers in the Valuation Office	690	690	690	615	615	615
Radiographers						
(a) where obliged to supply and launder their own white uniforms	242	242	242	242	242	242
(b) where obliged to supply their own white uniforms but laundered free	143	143	143	143	143	143
(c) where white uniforms are supplied and laundered by hospital	73	73	73	73	73	73
Respiratory & Pulmonary Function Technicians	191	191	191	191	191	191
RTE National Symphony Orchestra	2,476	2,476	2,476	2,476	2,476	2,476
RTE Concert Orchestra	2,476	2,476	2,476			
Shipping						
British Merchant Navy						
Foreign-going trade:						
(a) First class passenger and cargo liners.						
Master	318	318	318	318	318	318
Chief officer, chief engineer, other officers, including pursers	318	318	318	318	318	318
Chief steward	318	318	318	318	318	318
Assistant steward	244	244	244	244	244	244
Carpenter	194	194	194	194	194	194
Other ranks	148	148	148	148	148	148
(b) Cargo-vessels, tankers, ferries						
Master	318	318	318	318	318	318
Chief officer, chief engineer, other officers, including pursers	318	318	318	318	318	318
Chief steward	318	318	318	318	318	318
Assistant steward	244	244	244	244	244	244
Carpenter	194	194	194	194	194	194
Other ranks	148	148	148	148	148	148
British home or coasting trade:						
Master	318	318	318	318	318	318

Chief officer, chief engineer, other officers, including pursers	318	318	318	318	318	318
Chief steward	318	318	318	318	318	318
Assistant steward	244	244	244	244	244	244
Carpenter	194	194	194	194	194	194
Other ranks	148	148	148	148	148	148
Mercantile marine officers and crews of Irish ships						
Foreign-going trade: cargo vessels						
Master	98	98	98	98	98	98
Chief officer, chief engineer, radio officer	90	90	90	90	90	90
Other officers including pursers	73	73	73	73	73	73
Chief steward	73	73	73	73	73	73
Assistant steward	55	55	55	55	55	55
Carpenter (to include tools)	55	55	55	55	55	55
Other ranks, including boys	37	37	37	37	37	37
Home trade:						
(a) Cross channel and continental						
Master	98	98	98	98	98	98
Chief officer, chief engineer, radio officer	90	90	90	90	90	90
Other officers, including pursers	73	73	73	73	73	73
Chief steward	73	73	73	73	73	73
Assistant steward	55	55	55	55	55	55
Carpenter (to include tools)	55	55	55	55	55	55
Other ranks including boys	37	37	37	37	37	37
(b) Coasting vessels						
Master	98	98	98	98	98	98
Chief officer, chief engineer, radio officer	90	90	90	90	90	90
Other officers, including pursers	73	73	73	73	73	73
Chief steward	73	73	73	73	73	73
Assistant steward	55	55	55	55	55	55
Carpenter (to include tools)	55	55	55	55	55	55
Other ranks, including boys	37	37	37	37	37	37
Shop Assistants						
(including supermarket staff, general shop workers, drapery and footwear assistants)	121	121	121	121	121	115
Surveyors employed by:						
Local Authorities	127	127	127	127	127	127
Civil Service	127	127	127	127	127	127
Coillte	127	127	127	127	127	127
Teachers						
Teachers [excluding guidance counsellors, third-level academic staff and physical education teachers]						
School principals	608	608	608	608	558	558
Other teachers	518	518	518	518	475	475
Part-time teacher (on full hours)	518	518	518	518	475	475
Part-time (not on full hours)	279	279	279	279	256	256
Guidance Counsellors						
(a) employed full-time in second level schools	518	518	518	518	475	475
(b) engaged mainly in teaching general subjects but also doing part-time guidance counselling (additional allowance)	126	126	126	126	115	115
Third level academic staff						

Professor, Heads of Schools/Departments	608	608	608	608	558	558
Senior lecturer	518	518	518	518	475	475
College lecturer	518	518	518	518	475	475
Assistant lecturer	518	518	518	518	475	475
Part-time lecturer (on full hours)	518	518	518	518	475	475
Part-time lecturer (not on full hours)	279	279	279	279	256	256
Physical education teachers						
(a) fully engaged in teaching P.E.	518	518	518	518	475	475
(b) engaged mainly in teaching general subjects but also doing part-time P.E. (additional allowance)	126	126	126	126	115	115
Veterinary Surgeons	337	337	337	337	337	337

NOTE: Expenses deductions to be apportioned on a time basis